J. Rainer Twiford received his Ph.D.
from the University of Mississippi. From
1977 to 1980 he served as director of the
Children's Services Program at Region I
Mental Health Center in Mississippi, a
diagnostic and treatment center for
children from infancy to age eighteen;
then from 1980 to 1981 he directed the
Monticello Child Development Clinic in
Charlottesville, Virginia. He is now studying law at the University of
Virginia in Charlottesville.

J. RAINER TWIFORD

MANAGING CHILDREN'S BEHAVIOR

*A Guide for Parents,
Teachers, Counselors, Coaches,
and All Others
Who Work with Children*

A SPECTRUM BOOK

Prentice-Hall, Inc., Englewood Cliffs, New Jersey 07632

Library of Congress Cataloging in Publication Data

Twiford, J. Rainer.
    Managing children's behavior.

    "A Spectrum Book."
    Includes index.
        1. Child rearing.   2. Behavior modification.
    I. Napierala, Joseph.   II. Title.
    HQ769.T837   1984   649'.64   83-24608
    ISBN 0-13-550633-6
    ISBN 0-13-550625-5 (pbk.)

ISBN 0-13-550633-6

ISBN 0-13-550625-5 {PBK.}

Editorial/production supervision by Elizabeth Torjussen
Cover design©1984 by Jeannette Jacobs
Cover illustration by April Blair Stewart
Manufacturing buyer: Doreen Cavallo

This book is available at a special discount when ordered in
bulk quantities. Contact Prentice-Hall, Inc., General
Publishing Division, Special Sales, Englewood Cliffs, N.J. 07632.

Prentice-Hall International, Inc., *London*
Prentice-Hall of Australia Pty. Limited, *Sydney*
Prentice-Hall Canada Inc., *Toronto*
Prentice-Hall of India Private Limited, *New Delhi*
Prentice-Hall of Japan, Inc., *Tokyo*
Prentice-Hall of Southeast Asia Pte. Ltd., *Singapore*
Whitehall Books Limited, *Wellington, New Zealand*
Editora Prentice-Hall do Brasil Ltda., *Rio de Janeiro*

CONTENTS

PREFACE

Many people contributed to this book. I would like to thank Joe Napierala for chapters two and seven. I also thank Lynne Lumsden for her patience and cooperation throughout the lengthy preparation. I am grateful to Marsha and Eleanor for their enduring affection. Finally, I thank my parents for their absolute selflessness.

For my parents,
"Tish" and Horace Twiford

one

HELPING CHILDREN GROW

Most people would agree that the effective management of children is one of the foremost challenges to today's adult; however, a large number of adults are ill-prepared to meet this challenge. Most people spend twelve to twenty years of formal preparation for a vocation or career, but receive virtually no formal training in the area of parenting. This book is for parents, teachers, counselors, physicians, nurses, coaches, ministers, and anyone else who would like to manage children more effectively.

Modern psychology has made substantial progress in discovering techniques for managing the behavior of children. These principles are reducible to simple explanations and are easily applicable to daily life. A primary purpose of this book is to assist the adult in translating these principles into effective action to enable children to grow to realize their fullest potential. This book should be viewed as a practical guide to teach children to behave in constructive, productive, and acceptable ways.

Expectations of today's children are increasingly complex, demanding, and rigorous. Children are expected to assimilate vast amounts of academic material at very early ages. Children face stiffer competition for prized positions in school, in arts, and on the playing field. They are required to demonstrate acceptable social behaviors that render them attractive to both peers and adults. Exceedingly difficult choices concerning drugs and alcohol confront them as early as elementary school. On a larger scale, they are expected to make prudent moral decisions in the face of a diluted and ever changing system of social values. The list of challenges to children is seemingly endless.

Similarly, adult roles are becoming more difficult and demanding. Adults must cope with the excruciating reality of modern economics, which limits the amount of time, energy, and other resources that they can give to their children. More effort is required to maintain a comfortable standard of living. Economic conditions, as well as social changes, have resulted in a higher percentage of women in the labor force. Moreover, a greater number of people are forced to move away from their extended families to find work. Thus, parents must discover alternative sources of support in rearing their children.

Adults are searching for rational information concerning effective parenting techniques in today's dismally complex and rapidly changing society. Perhaps the most widely used, if least reliable, source of information is derived from personal experience. Most people tend to rear children in a way that is similar to how they were treated. Traditional methods of childrearing vary with geographic location, socioeconomic level, religious preference, and other factors. Because childrearing practices are so deeply ingrained in culture and religion, considerable emotion is typically associated with discussions of childrearing philosophy.

For example, whereas many adults vehemently advocate spanking, others intensely oppose the practice. Not surprisingly, differences in childrearing philosophies are a leading source of marital conflict. This book attempts to provide systematic and reliable suggestions that may help to reduce the emotional chaos that surrounds discussions of discipline.

The first step in achieving a useful understanding of children is to consider the word *behavior*. Behavior simply refers to what children do; thus, behavior is observable. Common behaviors include crying, crawling, walking, talking, running, laughing, hitting, sucking, biting, scratching, and eating. Each of these behaviors can be measured in terms of responses that can be observed, counted, and timed. Focusing on specific behavior enables two or more adults to agree on what they see the children doing. Attitudes, fears, or wishes are not behaviors because they are not observable; they are merely implied from observation of behavior. Two or more adults are less likely to reach the same conclusions concerning attitudes or fears as opposed to simply reporting the children's behavior. For example, a child who says "I hate school" may consistently turn in superior work, smile throughout the day, and offer to help the teacher. Does such a child have a bad attitude about school? This question would most likely elicit little agreement among adults.

There are no techniques available to alter labels; however, current behavioral technology can be used to alter specific behaviors. A disadvantage of using labels involves their impact on the children's self-esteem. Children may begin to think of themselves as lazy or selfish, or in other negative terms, and may then behave in a manner consistent with the label. A program that encourages children to spend more time studying and cleaning their rooms, however, usually increases self-esteem. Labels are avoided. Reliable judgments are made only by means of reporting the observed behavior, not by making inferences about that behavior.

Frequently, negative labels are applied to children's undesirable behavior. A child may be labeled as lazy, stupid, aggressive, passive, mean, sensitive, and so on. However, focusing on specific behaviors rather than using labels is preferable. First, labels tend to sitgmatize children, thus producing poor self-esteem and feelings of inadequacy. Second, labeling creates a self-fulfilling prophecy in which children accommodate to the expectations expressed by the label. This point is illustrated by the child who does worse in school after being told that he is "dumb." Third, labels may be more revealing of the person who creates the label than of the child in question. For example, the child who is called "mean" may be scorned by the classroom teacher but praised by the boxing coach. Remember that children are not bad, mean, lazy, or dumb, although they may display behaviors that are characteristic of such labels. The behaviors are much more easily altered than are the stigmatizing, self-perpetuating labels.

Currently available psychological techniques may be extremely useful in altering the behavior of children. The concept of altering or modifying behavior is inherently threatening to members of a society that places great value on individual freedom and the right to determine one's own destiny. Adverse reactions to behavior-control techniques have restricted their use in schools, prisons, psychiatric settings, and other institutions. The reader is cautioned that all powerful instruments may be employed to serve both good and evil ends. It is the responsibility of each individual to use the techniques that are explained on the following pages to achieve productive and humane goals that will benefit the individual as well as society. The purpose of this book is not to restrict the freedom of children but to encourage them to live rich, meaningful, and productive lives.

I have presented practical suggestions that encourage desirable behavior and discourage undesirable behavior. Although there is disagreement regarding the desirability of certain behaviors, it is assumed that most parents want their children to be happy, healthy, and creative, to do well in school, to get along with their peers, and to cooperate with demands at home. The principles offered in this book will help to achieve these ends. They extend well beyond any particular set of values.

Children do not behave in certain ways merely because they are told or expected to do so. Ways of behaving are learned by means of complex interactions between the children and their environments. Most behavior is learned from such interactions and is limited only by the inherited physical potential of the child. Although a great deal of learning occurs during early childhood, behavior is continually changing throughout life. The ways that behaviors are learned make up the fundamental topics of this book.

The first five chapters focus on encouraging desirable behavior. Methods of acquiring new behaviors, maintaining learned behaviors, and increasing motivation are discussed. The reader should gain an appreciation for the tremendous power of positive incentives in influencing behavior.

Chapter six is concerned with methods of discouraging undesirable behavior. Specific techniques for decreasing or extinguishing undesirable behavior are presented. The pros and cons of spanking and other types of punishment are discussed.

The remainder of the book deals with appropriate management of such problems as temper tantrums, poor school performance, fighting, or refusal to follow instructions.

Extensive case examples are cited throughout. The reader is advised that the identities of these children and their families are sufficiently disguised so that any descriptions of actual people are purely coincidental.

two

RECOGNIZING AND KEEPING TRACK OF BEHAVIOR

The beginnings of the behavioral approach to solving problems occurred in the scientific laboratory. Because of this, a necessary part of any behavioral program involves the accurate specification and recording of the behavior of interest. Knowing how much progress is made, and whether or not we are successful in our efforts, is based on how well we keep track of day-to-day observations and actions. Failure to do so can create difficulties later on.

Accurately specifying the behavior we are interested in involves defining a unit of behavior that can be reliably observed by anyone who knows the definition. For example, good behavior in the grocery store is not accurately specified, because some confusion exists about just what good behavior means in that situation. For some, a child's looking at toys while Mom shops might be considered good, while others might prefer to have the child with them at all times. Personal values influence interpretations of behavior, making it necessary for us to focus directly on the *actions* that define a behavior. This direct emphasis on action makes behavioral definitions observable and, therefore, directly measurable. We should thus include in our definition the things we do or do not want to see happen.

An additional advantage of accurately learning to specify behavior is that it improves our general ability to clearly communicate expectations to our children and others around us. In the example of behavior while shopping, it is evident that instructions to "walk next to me until we get the things we want" are more informative than being told to "behave yourself while we are in the store." Teachers are particularly aware of how precisely defined learning objectives help to guide students' progress in academic areas. They are no less important in daily living.

In specifying behavior according to an observable action it is helpful to have an understanding of how actions can be described. In general, we can describe any behavior (or action) according to the three dimensions of (1) *frequency*, that is, how often it occurs; (2) *duration*, how long each single action lasts; and (3) *intensity*, how much energy the behavior exhibits. These dimensions can be used either alone or in combination, depending on what our needs may be in specifying a behavior. The various methods of reinforcement, extinction, and punishment can be seen as either increasing or decreasing the frequency, duration, or intensity of a particular behavior. A presentation and case example will be provided to illustrate how these dimensions can be used in a program to change behavior.

FREQUENCY

Perhaps the simplest method of documenting behavior is merely counting the number of times it occurs. There are several readily available data collection devices, such as mechanical counters similar to those used by golfers, which make it easier to keep an accurate count of a particular behavior. By definition, systematic attempts at behavioral change are viewed as influencing the frequency of occurrence of a behavior, thus making frequency data collection one of the most widely used measures for program assessments. Increases or decreases in how often a behavior occurs are evaluated before, during, and after a systematic program is devised to change the behavior in the desired direction. The following case example illustrates the use of frequency recording in a program to deal with fighting between a brother and sister.

> Steve, age five, and Laura, age three, were reported by their mother to be "constantly fighting and bickering back and forth." This behavior was reported to be particularly troublesome while in the car on the way to and from nursery school and while at the dinner table. The time spent in the car was usually twenty minutes each way (morning and afternoon). Dinnertime generally took about forty minutes each day. A frequency count of the number of episodes of fighting—defined as talking to each other in a louder than usual (conversational) tone of voice, and as touching the other without permission, leading to protest—was kept by the mother. A counter was used to enable the mother to record the behavior accurately while driving and while eating. She merely clicked the counter upon observing the behavior and later recorded the final count. The number of times fighting occurred was divided by the number of minutes in the situation to yield a *rate of response* or frequency per unit of time. The program called for the mother to give her children a piece of sugarless gum or a mint after a peaceful drive. The dinnertime procedure was similar, except that dessert, rather than gum or mints, was used. Data indicated that fighting decreased and conversation between the children increased by using this approach.

DURATION

From the preceding example it can be seen that frequency represents a generally adequate way of describing a behavior and allows accurate data collection capability. The use of frequency counts is recommended in those situations where a behavior has a specific beginning and ending point and generally occurs for a similar length of time at each occurrence. If a behavior has a specific beginning and ending point, but occurs for a different length of time on each occurrence, a measure of duration may be more useful. For example, if a child throws a tantrum that lasts five minutes on one occasion, but forty-five minutes on another occasion, the frequency count would reflect two occurrences; but the episodes are not really comparable. A measure of duration is a more accurate means of specifying changes in behavior. Duration recording involves measuring the amount of time a given unit of behavior lasts. It is a time-based measure, and our goals of increasing or decreasing behaviors are thus measures in time units, such as minutes or seconds. The following case example represents a program attempt that used duration as the dimension of interest.

> Fred, age six, was described by his parents as a procrastinator, who took forever to accomplish his daily tasks of dressing, tooth-brushing, and breakfast—usually because he would become involved in playing, examining something, or asking questions instead of doing his task. Fred's parents would often become angry, threaten Fred, and provoke an angry response in the course of trying to speed him up. Tension within the family rapidly escalated from that point. Initial assessment involved having the mother (or father, when he was primary caretaker) keep track of how long it took Fred to (1) get dressed, (2) brush his teeth, and (3) eat breakfast, after being told once to do these tasks. These initial time units served as baseline data that were used for evaluating the success of the program that was implemented.

A systematic program was devised to decrease the duration of procrastination. A set of reasonable time limits for each of the three tasks was agreed upon. The program procedure involved having the parents tell Fred to get dressed and, at the same time, setting a mechanical timer (egg timer) for a reasonable time limit. Fred's job was then to "beat the clock" by completing the task before the alarm sounded. If Fred was successful he would receive a point on a wall chart, and could later trade his points for special privileges. In addition, both parents praised Fred for his performance by saying "I really like it when we get things done on time." The time limits were gradually decreased until Fred was able to complete the activity within a time frame acceptable to both parents.

Eventually, the parents were able to discontinue the use of the egg timer and relied on informal checking, praise, and rewards to maintain Fred's performance.

INTENSITY

The dimension of intensity is perhaps the most subjective—therefore, ambiguous—method of measuring behavior. It is not generally used alone in program attempts, because notions of frequency and duration usually comprise one's judgment of intensity. For example, a behavior that occurred very often and lasted a long time would probably be judged as more intense than one that happened occasionally and lasted for a few seconds. However, in some cases, the intensity can be important. The amount of energy exerted in some instances of aggressive behavior can be a crucial measure. The following case example serves to illustrate the importance of intensity.

Ben, age five, had never presented a behavior problem and was a rather quiet, timid boy. Because of his nonassertive nature, other boys would often pick on him, and he would rarely defend himself when engaged in a dispute. Ben's father, a dynamic, athletic, assertive person, was concerned about the situation and taught his son to box, suggesting that he should learn to defend himself. Not long afterward, Ben's teacher requested a conference with his parents because of changes in Ben's behavior—notably an increase in fighting with others. She described several recent incidents in which he had bloodied the nose or cut the lip of male classmates while on the playground. She felt that he was inappropriately aggressive and was concerned about the drastic change in his behavior, noting that even a minor altercation would prompt Ben to react violently. It became apparent that Ben was enjoying his newly discovered ability to fight. He now seemed to solve all of his personal problems with a left jab and a right uppercut. He would often arrive home and relate instances of his fighting skill to his parents, who at first approved of such assertiveness. Fortunately, the situation was easily resolved by having Ben's father set more appropriate rules for fighting. Ben was instructed never to hit first, and to use verbal means to assert himself and express his displeasure with others. He and his father practiced this, just as they had practiced boxing. This simple approach served to reduce the intensity of Ben's aggressive behavior, and his generally calm, easygoing manner returned. He would occasionally fight, but would always respect the rules his father had taught him.

These examples illustrate how the dimensions of frequency, duration, and intensity are used as behavior descriptions in programs to increase or decrease the dimensions of behavior. The key point is that each dimension provides a means of measuring the behavior in question, which encourages objective assessment and evaluation of program results. In each of the examples a method of data collection was used to keep track of the behavior of interest. Following are some tips that should assist you in data collection:

1. *Try to record data as close as possible to the time and location of the behavior.* This point cannot be overemphasized

because of the limits of our capacity to remember. The use of counters or other mechanical aids helps to keep track of behavior while allowing a person to engage in other activity. Transfer of data can be done later without sacrificing accuracy.

Another method of making data collection easier is to plan ahead by making paper and pencil or charts available at the location where behavior is being observed. For example, a chart for toothbrushing should be kept in the bathroom. For programs that involve mealtime or bedtime behaviors, the recording materials should be located in the appropriate areas.

2. *When possible, let children record their own behavior.* This consideration is based on the well-documented notion that merely focusing on a particular behavior can cause changes in its occurrence. For example, many weight loss programs require participants to record what they eat, and that alone usually leads to a decrease in eating. Increasing awareness of one's own behavior is an essential component of any program, in that self-involvement is necessary for success.

3. *Consider the child's age in choosing a data collection scheme.* The age of the person whose behavior is the focus of change is an important factor to consider in developing graphs, charts, and other methods of keeping track of behavior. The time-honored star chart used by teachers of young children represents one means of visually representing data in an appealing way. Parents can use these kinds of charts in the home as well, and they are often particularly effective with younger children. Additional methods of increasing children's interest involves the use of age-appropriate rewards. Younger children enjoy colorful, tangible items, whereas older children may respond to more abstract devices for behavior change.

4. *Use the data collection process as a time to review progress and give feedback to the person involved.* Recording data may be done to provide a means of evaluation and review of progress. When behavior is performed according to planned

procedures, recording represents the perfect time to deliver your approval and encouragement for appropriate performance.

Most programs attempt to provide systematic delivery of reinforcers for behavior—positive results are directly related to how well the process is carried out. The systematic delivery of the consequences of behavior represents the major reason that behavior changes. Using recording to cue the delivery process is an excellent way to ensure that rewards and punishments are administered systematically. This helps to reduce the confusion that threatens to contaminate any program for behavior change.

CHARTING AND GRAPHING: SOME EXAMPLES

The method of data collection will differ, depending on several factors. In the beginning stage, record keeping is more narrative, with the purpose of identifying the possible influences on a behavior. Information of interest usually includes where and when the behavior occurred, what the behavior looked like, and what happened before and after it occurred. Such notes can help to identify possible approaches for use in changing behavior. An example of a behavior assessment sheet is presented in Figure 1. These initial data also form the baseline or preliminary level of behavior before intervention and before the program is developed.

Keeping track of ongoing behavior during the course of a program can be accomplished by constructing simple charts or graphs to record observations. Figure 2 shows a chart that can be used to record both positive and negative behavior for a one-day period. Space for a total of twelve behaviors is provided, with frequencies recorded at two-hour intervals. Figure 3 shows a form that is suitable for recording five behaviors over a monthly time period. Daily totals can be entered and both morning and afternoon intervals may be used. It should be noted

FIGURE 1
BEHAVIOR ASSESSMENT

NAME: _____

Date/Time	Location	Behavior Description	What Happened Before	What Happened After

that frequency, duration, and intensity data can be recorded on the forms by including the appropriate dimension in the definition of the behavior. For example, in Figure 3, the category of arguing with brother is recorded in terms of the number of times it occurred, while doing homework and watching television are recorded as the number of minutes spent in the activity. Temper tantrums are rated according to intensity, with the numbers signifying the amount of intervention necessary to control the behavior.

Another means of portraying data is by graphs. The decision to use a chart or graph is really a matter of preference. Some people prefer the visual portrayal of increases and decreases in behavior that a graph provides. Figure 4 is an example of a graph that portrays the frequency of temper tantrums for a child over a three-week period. The initial seven days represents a baseline level with a program of systematically ignoring the behavior beginning on day eight and lasting through day twenty-one. The two axes of a graph represent the behavior

FIGURE 2

RECORDING POSITIVE AND NEGATIVE BEHAVIOR

NAME: _____ DATE: _____

Behaviors	A.M. 7-9	9-11	11-1	P.M. 1-3	3-5	5-7	7-9	9-11	Total
P 1.									
O 2.									
S 3.									
I 4.									
T									
I 5.									
V 6.									
E									
Totals									
N 1.									
E 2.									
G 3.									
A 4.									
T									
I 5.									
V 6.									
E									
Totals									

FIGURE 3
OBSERVATION DAYS

DATE: NAME:

Behavior	Time	Su	M	T	W	Th	F	S	Su	M	T	W	Th	F	S	Su	M	T	W	Th	F	S
Arguing with brother	A.M.	3	4	6	7																	
	P.M.	6	4	2																		
Watching television (P.M. only) in minutes	A.M.																					
	P.M.	60	120	30	75	50	120	60														
Time spent doing homework	A.M.																					
	P.M.	10	15	10	20	20	0	0	30													
Temper tantrum intensity 0 = no behavior 1 = verbal warning 2 = sent to room	A.M.	2	2	2	2	0	1	1	1													
	P.M.	1	1	1	0	0	0	2	0													
	A.M.																					
	P.M.																					

FIGURE 4

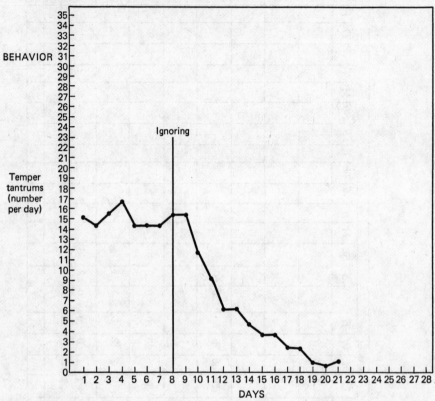

description, with the vertical axis generally representing the behavior measurement and the horizontal axis representing the time frame of the program.

Familiarize yourself with these scientific methods of observing behavior. Practice using them to record your own behavior. Also, keep these ideas in mind while reading the rest of this book. It is essential to be able to record and observe behavior objectively in order to manage it effectively.

The value of these records lies in their availability for comparing the effectiveness of various strategies that you choose in altering your child's behavior. You will be able to determine whether or not a strategy is effective by comparing various sets of objective data that you have recorded. In this way, effective techniques may be continued and applied to other behaviors, while ineffective strategies can be discarded or modified.

three

REWARDING
BEHAVIOR

I was once asked, "How is it possible for one child to become a minister, one a doctor, and another a habitual criminal, when all were reared by the same parents?" The answer to this question lies at the heart of several fundamental issues of modern psychology. It is reasonably safe to say that these differences are not caused predominantly by the inherited or genetic constitutions of the three children. Children often show distinct personalities at birth (before a great deal of learning takes place); however, such characteristics are readily susceptible to environmental influence. Most psychologists would stress the role of motivation and learning in attempting to answer the question. Motivation may generally be referred to as a force that causes one to act in a certain directed manner. Motivation is shaped by experience and the ways in which it is learned will be discussed in the following two chapters.

POSITIVE REINFORCEMENT

Everyone knows that the anticipation of rewards, in addition to the actual rewards, has considerable influence on the way people behave. The working adult may be rewarded by praise, satisfaction of a job well done, money, opportunity for advancement, recognition, or merely by having something interesting to do. Such incentives provide the motivation to work hard and perform to the best of one's ability. If the working environment is devoid of such rewards or incentives, the adult may lose motivation and begin turning in poor quality work, miss work, or look for another job.

Rewards operate in much the same way for children. Although children may not be aware of the process, they will work very hard to get the things that they want. Psychologists did not discover this seemingly obvious principle; however, they have studied, refined, and tested it scientifically. Psychologists have found that when certain objects or events are presented immediately following a behavior, behavior is more likely to reoccur. This procedure is called *positive reinforcement*. We typically think of these objects or events as rewards; yet, for the sake of clarity, they are called *reinforcers*—that is, they reinforce the preceding behavior. The most effective method of increasing the strength of a desirable behavior is to present a reinforcer after the behavior occurs. As you will see, this apparently simple idea can become quite complex.

There are a variety of potential reinforcers that are available in the children's immediate environment. Reinforcers that satisfy the basic physical needs of children are called *primary reinforcers* and include food, water, shelter, or environmental stimulation. Items, such as money or tokens, that can be exchanged for primary reinforcers are called *secondary reinforcers*. The application of reinforcers can be very useful in maintaining desired behavior once the children have learned the association between the type of reinforcers and the behavior involved.

Another group of effective reinforcers, which include kisses, hugs, praise, a pat on the head, or other kinds of attention, are *social reinforcers*. Each of the types of reinforcers should be used in combination to strengthen and maintain a desirable behavior.

The effectiveness of reinforcers may vary considerably among children. Obviously, a trip to the pizza parlor would have little value to a child who has just finished supper, and a daily allowance would not motivate the child who has not learned the value of money. Finding effective reinforcers may require some imagination and periods of trial and error. It is often helpful simply to ask the child what he or she would like to work toward.

To ensure optimal effectiveness, it is necessary to consider the amount of a particular reinforcer. It is not always true that large quantities of a reinforcer, such as money or praise, provide the greatest incentive values for children. For example, two boxes of raisins may be no more effective than one box in reinforcing a child's behavior for emptying the garbage. The adult must exercise caution by not administering too much of one type of reinforcer, such that the child does not become quickly satiated. This can be prevented by varying both the amount and kind of reinforcer applied to a specific behavior.

Timing of the reinforcer is also critical to its effectiveness. Consider the following examples:

Four-year-old Janey was experiencing difficulty in learning to clean her room without constant reminding. One morning Janey surprisingly took the initiative to straighten her bed and put her toys in the closet where she was told they belonged. Mom was pleased so she called Dad at the office to tell him. The same afternoon, Janey was arguing with her younger sister when Dad arrived. Taking no particular notice of the situation, he declared, "Janey, I'm so proud of you that I bought the game that you wanted." Janey initiated several more arguments before bedtime.

Nine-year-old Bobby's father offered him two dollars if he would make the honor roll at the end of the six-week grading period. Bobby liked the idea because he wanted to buy a new reel for his fishing rod, so he studied diligently for the first week. Thereafter, he decided that he would rather spend his evenings watching television.

Reinforcers should be presented immediately following the desired behavior to produce the optimal effect. In the first illustration, Janey was actually reinforced for arguing with her sister; therefore, arguing rather than cleaning her room was the behavior that was reinforced. For Bobby, the delay in obtaining the reel was too long to reinforce studying behavior effectively. A more immediate reinforcer, such as the opportunity to watch television after studying for one hour, would more likely have produced the desired effect. Immediate reinforcers, such as television viewing, used in combination with long-term incentives, such as the fishing reel, would act as powerful motivators for studying behavior. Immediate reinforcement is particularly essential in strengthening behavior in young children. Delays between the behavior and the application of the reinforcer teach patience and persistence to older children and young adults. Consider the delay of gratification that faces first-year medical students. The adult must be careful not to stretch the delay to the point that the child's motivation to work diminishes. Words of praise and encouragement certainly help to extend the period of allowable delay.

Throughout the initial stages of learning a new behavior, reinforcers should be presented lavishly after each occurrence of the specified behavior. Fewer reinforcers of a lesser quantity are required to maintain a behavior once it has been well-established. Thus, the behavior may be maintained on a lean schedule of reinforcement. This simply refers to the fact that well-established behavior will continue at a high rate even though reinforcement may be administered infrequently or in small amounts. The adult may choose to reinforce the behavior a certain fixed number of times after the desired behavior occurs or may simply choose to reinforce the behavior subsequent to an average number of occurrences, thus varying the application of the reinforcer. A trial-and-error approach is suggested in determining when and how much of a reinforcer should be delivered. The general rule is that reinforcers should be given more often and in greater quantities in the initial stages of a program. The frequency and quantity should be gradually reduced as long as the child shows continued interest in working for the reinforcer.

There are many important cues that help children learn to discriminate among the appropriate times and places to exhibit various behaviors. For example, a teacher standing at the front of a classroom is usually a cue for the child to pay attention. A playground equipped with swings and a sliding board is usually a cue to engage in physical activity. Such cues are obvious to most children and tend to elicit the expected behavior. However, there are many occasions when there are no clearly discriminable cues that tell the child how to behave. Novel events, such as taking a field trip, riding an airplane, or attending a family reunion, may confuse the unprepared child. Adults should clearly enunciate their expectations of the child at such events. Specific guidelines or rules of behavior should be discussed in great detail. The child should also be made to understand the consequences of appropriate as well as inappropriate behavior and should then expect such consequences to be delivered accordingly. These suggestions may seem obvious to most adults; however, cues for desirable behavior are often less apparent to children. Many adults have experienced or can imagine being lost in a strange city inhabited by people who speak an unfamiliar language. Surely children experience similar feelings when thrown into novel situations without proper cues for appropriate behavior.

Before closing the discussion concerning strengthening and maintaining desirable behaviors, I would like to dispel several myths associated with positive reinforcement. Parents often confuse positive reinforcement with bribery. A more careful examination of the word *bribe* should put this matter to rest. The following is a common dictionary (*Webster's New World*) definition of *bribe*: " . . . anything given or promised as an inducement to do something illegal or wrong. . . ." The word *bribe* simply does not apply to a procedure that involves reinforcing appropriate behavior. Another misconception concerns the belief that children demand more frequent rewards for a greater variety of behaviors after a reinforcement program is established. Actually, the opposite is true—once the behavior is established, fewer incentives are required to maintain it. The behavior often becomes rewarding in and of itself. Furthermore, many people confuse reinforcement with coaxing. Children's parents may coax them to be in bed at a certain hour. The child actually receives more attention for displaying the undesirable behavior (staying up) than for the desirable behavior (going to bed on time). For this illustration, positive reinforcement would involve the presentation of a reinforcer, such as praise, if the child were in bed by the designated time.

In conclusion, positive reinforcement is a powerful learning technique that can encourage desirable behavior or inadvertently strengthen undesirable behavior. Positive reinforcement is limited only by the potential of the child. Obviously, most children do not have the capacity to become Nobel Prize recipients, Olympic medalists, or outstanding novelists. Given these limitations, effective use of reinforcement principles can motivate children to make the best use of their inherited abilities.

NEGATIVE REINFORCEMENT

A procedure that is often confused with punishment is *negative reinforcement*. Remember that any reinforcement technique increases behavior, whereas punishment decreases behavior.

The removal of an aversive stimulus serves to increase the probability of behavior that occurs before the stimulus is removed.

Two examples of negative reinforcement are avoidance and escape. Children may work arduously to avoid a spanking, loss of their allowances, or critical remarks from their peers. They will seek to prevent the application of an aversive stimulus or situation. Likewise, escape behavior is reinforced when it removes a child from an ongoing aversive stimulus. A simple example of escape might involve leaving a room that is too hot or too cold. Another example would be running away from home or school. A child may experience a sense of relief subsequent to escaping from an abusive parent or unpleasant teacher.

Most behavior is managed more efficiently by employing positive, as opposed to negative, reinforcement techniques. Adults should encourage children to work *for* privileges rather than to *avoid* punishment. Punishment may involve the application of an aversive stimulus or the removal of a privilege.

CONCLUSION

Reinforcement principles are critical in determining the kinds of behavior that children will eventually display. Skillful application of reinforcement principles can increase the likelihood of your children's engaging in healthy and constructive activities. Lack of awareness of (or well-intentioned misuse of) these contingencies may encourage an array of surprisingly resilient, undesirable behaviors.

four

LEARNING
NEW SKILLS

SHAPING

The process of reinforcing, thus strengthening, existing desirable behaviors was the primary topic of the preceding chapter. Variations of these procedures, as well as other techniques that are used in the acquisition of new skills, are discussed in this chapter. One valuable technique that is used in helping a child learn new behaviors is called *shaping* (a technical term for a method of successive approximations). The first step in designing a shaping program involves establishing a behavioral goal. Specific goals, or *target behaviors*, include examples such as making a phone call, writing a letter, cleaning the kitchen, or hitting a curve ball. Each of these skills is comprised of a succession of specific behaviors that are mastered before the target behavior is achieved. Small steps, or approximations, toward mastery of the target behavior must be amply rewarded. As many casual observers of child development have noted, children must learn to walk before they can run.

Consider the following examples:

Eleven-year-old Sandra wanted to learn to play tennis, but had never held a racket. Her instructor set a goal for her to return ninety percent of the balls within the first three months of instruction. To test her current ability, the instructor found that Sandra could return only five percent of the balls hit to her. Sandra was then shown the correct grips for forehand, backhand, and serve. She was lavishly praised for successful strokes. Subsequently, Sandra was taught the appropriate stance that involved bending her knees and stepping into the ball with her side toward the net. Again, she was tested and praised each time she correctly demonstrated her newly acquired skills. She could return thirty percent of the shots at that point. Sandra was experiencing difficulty in keeping her eye on the ball while concentrating on the other skills, so she was instructed to practice stroking an imaginary ball. After mastering the grip, stance, and swing, Sandra was told to concentrate solely on watching the ball. This new skill, focusing on the ball, combined with the other skills, allowed her to return sixty percent of the balls. She practiced and refined all the skills and experienced a pleasant sense of accomplishment each time she made a good shot. She added spins, drop shots, and lobs to her repertoire and was returning ninety-two percent of the balls after ten weeks of intensive practice.

Five-year-old Donald was reported to withdraw from others and engage in solitary play for the entire play period. Donald's teacher set a goal for him to play cooperatively with the other children for a minimum of thirty minutes each day. First, the teacher administered raisins and praises each time she observed him watching the other children. Next, Donald was rewarded each time he moved closer to another child, although the behavior was initially unintentional. He began to consistently move closer to other children, yet no true interaction was observed. He was then rewarded each time he spoke to another child, and the children were encouraged to initiate conversation with him. Donald began to interact spontaneously with his peers after seven weeks of training. Mutual, cooperative play soon became highly reinforcing itself; hence, no further training was necessary.

The two examples serve to demonstrate simple shaping procedures. Each example includes several common elements that are required to render the technique effective. First, a measurable goal or target behavior was defined. Second, the child's current behavior was observed and noted. Small steps toward achieving the goal were vigorously reinforced in order to enhance the child's motivation for continuing in that activity. Once the goal was achieved, the activity was found to be self-sustaining because of the acquired value of the new skill.

Complex behaviors, such as writing letters, performing algebraic equations, or driving a car, usually require years of shaping. The requisite skills for these activities tend to build on each other in a pyramidal fashion. Achievement of the target behavior requires demonstrated competence of more fundamental skills. For example, a child must know how to add, subtract, multiply, and divide numbers before doing algebra. It is essential to practice and master basic requisite skills of a target behavior before attempting to demonstrate that behavior. Therefore, the parent, teacher, or coach should have an explicit understanding of the various requisite skills that comprise a particular target behavior. Such understanding is best achieved by a careful analysis of all the skills that are required for successful demonstration of the target behavior. The procedure is sometimes referred to as a *task analysis*.

IMMEDIATE FEEDBACK

It is important to offer a child immediate feedback for behavior. This vital information serves as both reference and reinforcer for correct responding. New skills are acquired more efficiently when the child is immediately aware of the correctness of the response. Correct responding is rewarded and incorrect responding is adjusted immediately subsequent to the feedback. Immediate feedback is applied to behavior in a variety of situations, including academic, athletic, and social behavior.

The value of immediate feedback is most widely recognized with regard to *programmed instruction*. Programmed instruction methods typically break large amounts of material into smaller components. The child is given the opportunity to rehearse a new skill or knowledge as it is learned in small steps. For example, a small amount of information may be visually presented to the child and a question concerning that material may follow in the text. The child would answer the question and be immediately informed of the accuracy of the response. The child may proceed to advanced material once he or she has mastered the more simple material.

FADING

Fading is a technique that involves the performance of an established behavior in the presence of a changing stimulus or set of circumstances. In this way, the child acquires a new skill without the frustration of making mistakes throughout the learning process. Therefore, fading is sometimes called errorless discrimination. Consider the following examples:

> Buddy is the star forward on the high school basketball team, although he has shown little ability at the free-throw line. He made only thirty-six percent of his free throws and his team was defeated in several close games as a result of his missing crucial

free throws. The school psychologist was aware of the problem and offered to help. An adjustable goal was procured so that Buddy could practice shooting at a lower height. He was also instructed to stand closer to the goal while shooting two hundred practice shots daily. A record of his shooting percentage was kept and he was found to make eighty-eight percent of the baskets. Every third day the goal was raised six inches and Buddy was placed one foot farther from the goal. He was gradually moved back to the official foul line with the goal again raised to normal height (ten feet) and continued to shoot with above seventy-five percent accuracy. This improvement was also observed during the game situation and the team showed a more successful record thereafter.

Megan is a five-year-old who was having considerable difficulty learning to write her name. She was given a paper with her name written in bold print with a magic marker. A piece of typing paper was placed over the printed material to enable Megan to trace her name. Subsequent to tracing against the bold print she was given a finer copy that was written with a ball-point pen to trace. She practiced tracing the finer copy for two days and subsequently was able to write her name on a blank piece of paper without tracing.

The above examples of fading techniques have several common elements. New skills are acquired by adjusting the stimulus in the presence of a behavior that already exists in the child's repertoire. Hence the technique involves practicing and refining skills that are observed on a rudimentary level. The stimulus is gradually faded such that the task becomes more difficult, yet the level of the child's accuracy in responding remains constant. This is a success-oriented approach to learning that facilitates confidence and minimizes the experience of frustration that children often encounter in learning new skills.

CUEING

The importance of teaching children to discriminate among

times, places, and situations was mentioned briefly in the previous chapter. This topic will be considered in more detail.

Eight-year-old Sandra was recently prescribed glasses—much to her chagrin. She initially refused to wear them until her parents became insistent that she do so. They initiated several disciplinary actions, such as turning off the television, sending her to her room, and scorning her whenever she was observed without her glasses. She began to wear them at home; however, her teacher reported that she had never worn them at school.

Thirteen-year-old Bobby was the city's champion boxer in his age division. He was praised by his coaches and opponents for his quick hands and fluid style. Yet Bobby was not popular with his peers because he would playfully jab and punch them continually. His peers avoided him in the halls, the lunchroom, and on the playground.

Seven-year-old Kathy was referred to Dr. Miller, a psychologist, because she was extremely shy and withdrawn. Kathy refused to interact with Dr. Miller and would hide her face behind her hands. As a result of reinforcement and shaping procedures, Kathy gradually began to communicate appropriately with Dr. Miller. However, the teacher reported no improvement at school.

As children grow and mature they become increasingly capable of discriminating among various cues in the environment. Newborn infants respond in virtually the same way to all stimuli. Increased motor activity is observed in response to sights, sounds, odors, or skin pressure. In time, babies begin to respond quite differently to various stimuli. The ability to respond in a sophisticated, discriminating manner usually increases with the age and intelligence of the child. This ability is learned; therefore, proper training should facilitate successful discrimination.

The foregoing case examples illustrate the importance of discriminating among appropriate times and places for various behaviors. External cues, such as verbal reminders, lists, and facial expressions, are initially essential in eliciting desirable behavior. These cues should be gradually replaced by the child's set of internal cues that include thinking, imagery, and emotion. Hence cues should be presented externally while learning appropriate behavior, and internal cues will gradually become sufficient to elicit the correct response.

All cues should be presented in a direct and straightforward manner. Examples of direct cues include the following:

> Sandra, always wear your glasses at school. You will be allowed to watch television tonight only if your teacher tells us that you wore your glasses all day.

> Bobby, you must fight only in the boxing ring. You will be suspended from the boxing team for one week if you are seen hitting anyone outside of the ring.

These are direct cues that clearly explain the expected behavior and its consequences. Examples of indirect cueing might include:

> It is hard for you to see without your glasses.

> People don't like it when you punch them.

These cues do not clearly elucidate expected behavior, nor do they point out consequences. Desired changes in behavior are not encouraged by nebulous and indirect cues. However, these indirect cues may serve as reminders once the behavior is well-established.

An important issue to consider when teaching children to respond to appropriate cues is whether or not training will generalize from one setting to another. We saw that Kathy learned to interact appropriately with Dr. Miller; however, this behavior did not generalize to her "natural" environment. Behavior tends to occur primarily in the settings where reinforcers are applied to that behavior. Thus, reinforcing a particular behavior in a variety of settings will help to ensure that the behavior occurs in many situations. Kathy should be praised and rewarded for interacting with her siblings at home and with her peers at school. More specific cues are usually required for interacting in the classroom. For example, talking in class is usually desirable only if the teacher explicitly gives permission to do so. Otherwise, the behavior is inappropriate and reinforcers for it should be eliminated. This can be achieved by separating the students who are talking, by ignoring the talking, or by asking the child to leave the room.

Cues range from disarmingly simple to overwhelmingly complex. Consider the eight-month-old who responds to a person's leaving by waving "bye-bye." This represents a very simple cue for a simple response. On the other hand, a sixteen-year-old violinist producing changes in tempo, volume, and other qualities of music in response to the hand signals of the maestro represents responding to an exquisitely complex set of stimuli. Efforts should be made to coordinate the level of difficulty of the cue with the age and ability of the child. As discussed in the shaping and fading sections of this chapter, simple skills are building blocks for more complex and sophisticated behavior.

five

IMPROVING
ACADEMIC
PERFORMANCE

Educating today's youth is one of the most crucial and difficult tasks that faces modern society. Considering underpaid teachers, racial strife, student violence, pervasive use of drugs in the schools, assembling of diverse and heterogeneous populations by arduous bus travel, and other problems that confront the educational system, it is more important than ever that parents help their children to achieve in school. Methods of helping children achieve their fullest academic potential are explored here.

Reports of the tightening job market for college graduates and unemployed holders of Ph.D. degrees abound in the press. The popular notion that a technical vocation is more fruitful than a white-collar, professional position has flourished. Although there are many exceptions, level of education continues to correlate with reported job satisfaction and level of income. Individuals with the highest academic degrees from the best schools are usually selected for the choice positions in the job market. It should be noted that education yields many benefits that are not directly related to career preparation. A solid education should facilitate an individual's ability to solve complex problems with the tools of rational, systematic thinking, coupled with a rich fund of general information. Education serves to sharpen one's sensitivity to aesthetics and increase appreciation for the arts. Well-educated individuals hold a better intellectual grasp of international affairs because of their ability to perceive events in a historical context. These and other by-products of education improve adaptability to a variety of situations.

INTELLIGENCE

Academic performance is determined by two general components: *intelligence* and *motivation.* From the psychologist's point of view, intelligence is an extremely complex and controversial topic. Definitions of intelligence vary widely among psychologists. It is sometimes referred to as the ability to behave in an adaptive manner. Others contend that intelligence is the ability to employ abstract and logical reasoning, while some say that intelligence is simply that which is measured by an intelligence test.

Intelligence tests are designed to measure a number of abilities that are required in academic settings. For example, measures of vocabulary, memory, judgment, reasoning, perception, motor coordination, and problem solving abilities are usually obtained. A combination of these and other factors yields a score (IQ). The intelligence quotient theoretically represents the general intelligence level of the child. The two most widely used individual tests are the *Stanford-Binet Intelligence Scale* and the *Wechsler Intelligence Scale for Children—Revised.*

Many critics of intelligence testing assert that the tests are designed for middle-class, white children. For this reason, the tests discriminate against minorities and other children who do not share similar cultural backgrounds. Hence, the fact that black children on the average score fifteen points lower on the tests is interpreted as a deficiency in the test because of its culturally discriminatory properties. Racial differences in IQ have been the focus of heated academic debates concerning whether such differences are of genetic or environmental origin. The debate will likely continue for many years to come.

Despite the controversy surrounding intelligence testing, IQ tests serve a useful function in modern society. The scores serve as reasonably good predictors of academic performance. Specific intellectual strengths and weaknesses are pinpointed, thus enabling a teacher to design educational programs that capitalize on intellectual strengths. However, the IQ test should never be used as the sole instrument for determining school placement.

We know that IQs represent inherited as well as acquired ability. The genetic make-up of an individual may serve to impose an upper limit to the level of intellectual functioning that can be achieved. The nature of the infant's environment, the richness of intellectual activity within the home, the quality of the school system, and other environmental variables interact to determine whether or not the inherited potential is realized.

Psychologists have placed considerable emphasis on the role of environment in the development of intelligence throughout the past two decades. Studies suggest that early experience is crucial in determining IQ. One scientist even found differences in the brain chemistry of rats that were exposed to enriched, stimulating environments. In reaction to studies that emphasized the importance of the environment, the government initiated preschool enrichment programs, such as Head Start. Recent evaluations of these programs have yielded disappointing results. Several explanations are offered for the failure of the programs significantly to increase and sustain IQ. First, the quality of the intervention is questionable. Many programs serve as day-care and nutritional support centers rather than intellectual enrichment programs. Second, intervention did not begin early enough. Many scientists assert that irreversible deficiencies in cognitive development may exist by age three, at which time most children enter enrichment programs. Third, enrichment activities are typically terminated when the child enters the public school system. Enrichment activities should continue for many years. Finally, many researchers contend that early enrichment should focus on making permanent alterations in the home environment. Hence, the child development specialist should endeavor to engage parents as well as siblings in the enrichment process.

Such findings have several important implications for parents. Children should be provided with an interesting and stimulating environment. For infants, it is important to stimulate the senses by encouraging exploration. Infants should be allowed to touch, taste, hear, see, and smell a wide variety of stimuli. Verbal interaction becomes increasingly important with age. Telling bedtime stories and reading to children are often interesting activities even before the child is capable of comprehending the messages. Music is exciting and enjoyable to most children. Games that increase coordination and awareness of spatial relations, such as building blocks, puzzles, and crayons should be available to young children. The toys do not have to be expensive. Creative parents and children can discover numerous ways of using ordinary household items for exploratory play.

Perhaps the most important ingredient of enrichment is the quality and extent of adult supervision. Although solitary play and interaction with peers are recommended activities, supervision of sensitive and caring adults is crucial in enhancing cognitive development.

MOTIVATION

Children with equal ability often do not demonstrate equal academic achievement. Discrepancies in academic performance are largely caused by differences in motivation. The motivation to achieve in school is acquired by associations with parents, teachers, and peers. The motivated child tends to come from middle- and upper-class families who encourage academic success and who, themselves, engage in intellectual activities such as reading, art, and music appreciation or professional activities. Further encouragement is offered by peers from similar backgrounds. Consider the following comment concerning the environmental context of motivation:

> From school entrance on, middle and upper-class parents typically display a marked interest in their children's academic careers—urging greater effort, praising indications of progress, and, not infrequently, providing "more tangible rewards, in the form of movies, bicycles, or spending money for accomplishments in school." These parents are likely to view education as the solution to a wide range of economic, social, and personal problems. . . . Parents of academically motivated, achieving children are likely to place a high value on autonomy and independence, rather than dependence and conformity, and on mastery, competence, and achievement generally. These parents tend to be democratic and to encourage an active "give-and-take" interaction with their children; they exhibit curiosity and a respect for knowledge. In contrast, parental dominance of the child, particularly maternal dominance, and parental submissiveness both adversely affect the development of autonomy and achievement motivation. (P.H. Mussen, J.J. Conger, and J. Kagan, *Child Development and Personality* [New York: Harper & Row, 1974], pp. 503-505).

The foregoing serves as a general description of the environment of the motivated child, although there are large differences in parenting practices and environments of motivated children. Now we will turn our attention toward specific methods of increasing motivation.

Considerable emphasis on making good grades exists in most school systems. Advancement in school, admission to college, admission to graduate and professional schools, and entry into the work force are all, to some extent, contingent on grades achieved in school. For this reason, most parents are concerned about their children's school performance. Hence rewards and punishments are often distributed according to the attainment of good grades. Privileges, such as television time, favorite desserts, and spending money, are exchanged for favorable reports. The parent is responsible for ensuring that homework assignments are complete and acceptable. Rewards should be applied when children bring assignments and materials home and complete the homework independently. For optimal results, home study should occur in the afternoon, after school, such that rewarding events (supper and recreation time) follow the study period. Remember that it is necessary to present reinforcement after the occurrence of the desired behavior, not before. Also, children usually seem to enjoy their recreational time more if all of the day's work is complete. This principle is sometimes referred to as *utility of leisure.* Many parents argue that children deserve a rest after school and that homework should be done in the evenings. From my observations, these parents struggle a great deal more with their children over getting homework done.

Through praise, encouragement, and tangible rewards, children learn to perform the activities that generally lead to good grades. Many parents voice the following complaint: "Why should I have to give my children rewards to get them to do the things they should do anyway?" This is a question of principle and child-rearing philosophy. The approach taken here is more practical, in that the emphasis is on increasing the desired activity. Children may simply fail to see the intrinsic value of doing well in school. However, the likelihood that they will learn to appreciate the value of education will increase once they begin to perform successfully in school. To take the argument a step further, assume that individuals should contribute to society by working—then remove pay and other rewards for work because we *expect* the job to be done. How many of us would continue working?

Any time that adults set about changing a child's behavior, both child and adult should agree on specific goals. Within an academic setting, the goal should be not to attain certain grades but to perform routinely activities that yield good grades. Goals should be moderately difficult to achieve. Goals that are too difficult or too easy to attain generate minimal achievement motivation. Attainment of the goal should always be a satisfying experience, with coveted achievement rewards. Many behaviors have natural rewards, such as the prestige and satisfaction associated with creating a winning science fair project. Natural reinforcers within the academic sphere are primary motivators for achieving; however, most younger children initially require extrinsic rewards to perform to the best of their abilities.

CONCLUSION

Successful school performance generally depends on two factors: intelligence and motivation to achieve. Intelligence is derived from a combination of genetic and experiential factors. Motivation is derived solely from experience. Suggestions are offered for creating an environment that enhances ability and motivation.

six

MANAGING
UNDESIRABLE
BEHAVIOR

Perhaps the topic of decreasing undesirable behavior inspires more controversy than any other child-rearing issue. Traditional Judeo-Christian principles emphasize the role of punishment in child-rearing. Punishment usually refers to the application of harsh and aversive consequences to a wrongful deed. This procedure typically serves as retribution for a misdeed and discourages future tendencies to engage in the undesirable act. The value of punishment has been so overemphasized that the word *punishment* is often mistakenly used synonymously with *discipline*. I have often heard adults speak of parents who do not spank their children in the following way: "Bob is difficult to manage. You know his parents don't discipline him."

Psychologists and other behavioral scientists have investigated the effects of punishment on children's development. The results of the studies suggest that punishment may often result in serious, undesirable side effects. Perhaps the most serious objection to physical punishment has been that it may encourage or lead to child abuse. Although limited and appropriate use of punishment may be useful, psychologists encourage adults to search for more positive and effective alternatives to discipline. A large segment of modern society is responsive to the notion of positive discipline. These progressive-thinking adults were euphemistically labeled "the permissive society" by the more traditional and conservative religious groups. Increases in juvenile crimes, drug use, and violence have been attributed to the lenient child-rearing practices of the permissive society, even though no evidence exists to support such ideas. Parents and teachers have been called on to reinstate discipline (that is, corporal punishment) as a means of inculcating order, respect for authority, and moral behavior in today's youth.

I will attempt to discuss objectively the effects of punishment procedures in this chapter. Advantages, disadvantages, and alternatives to punishment will be explored. I hope to demonstrate that the use of positive alternatives to discipline is not the same as permissiveness.

DEFINITION

The technical definition of punishment is somewhat different from the lay definition. Punishment in a technical sense refers to any procedure that decreases the probability of a behavior. Usually, an aversive stimulus or situation, called a punisher, is administered subsequent to an undesirable behavior. This tends to suppress or decrease the probability of the future occurrence of that behavior. The person who administers the punisher is called the punishing agent.

Effective punishers vary widely among individuals. A

stimulus that is punishing to one individual may be highly reinforcing to another. An extreme illustration of this point involves individuals who engage in sadomasochistic behavior as a pleasurable and sexually gratifying experience. The vast majority of individuals view this behavior as aversive, punitive, and noxious. The most common punishers applied to undesirable behaviors in children include slapping, spanking, scolding, lecturing, blaming, criticizing, and removal of privileges. All of these punishers have been applied to the undesirable behavior of children at one time or another.

There is significant variability in the behaviors that are considered to be undesirable and deserving of a punishment procedure. A list of commonly cited undesirable behaviors might include hitting, cursing, stealing, wetting and soiling, lying, crying, and so on. However, there may be little or no consensus among adults with regard to the desirability of a particular behavior. For example, one parent might encourage fighting in certain situations, whereas another might be inclined to punish the child for the same behavior. A crucial aspect of effective management is achieving some agreement or consistency concerning the desirability of behavior and the use of punishment procedures. This can be achieved through calm and rational discussion that involves all of the adults who are responsible for discipline. It is also important to include the child in discussions of discipline whenever possible.

PHYSICAL PUNISHMENT

Janey is a nine-month-old who is a "fussy" baby. Janey's mother is seventeen years old and becomes extremely frustrated in response to Janey's frequent crying episodes. She applies three or four swats to her rear end in an attempt to stop the crying.

Susan is a thirteen-month-old who recently learned to walk. At first she enjoyed walking up to the coffee table in her living room and exploring the attractive, colorful items displayed there. Susan's mother would firmly slap her hand and say "no" whenever Susan reached for one of the items. Susan grew less likely to explore interesting and colorful objects thereafter.

William is a first grader who has never been spanked. During the first week of school he ran into the street to catch the school bus without first looking for traffic. Fortunately, there were no cars nearby. His father observed the incident, and William was soundly spanked for his behavior and lectured about the necessity of stopping to look for traffic. Thereafter, William always paused at the curb to look both ways.

Frank is a five-year-old who would often throw temper tantrums and refuse to obey his mother's requests. She had three other children to manage, and Frank's behavior infuriated her. One day she became so frustrated and angry that she began vigorously to spank Frank. As she hit him she grew more angry and escalated the intensity of the beating to the point that serious physical damage resulted. Frank was rushed to the hospital by a neighbor and treated in the Pediatric Intensive Care Unit. His mother was charged with child abuse and she lost custody of Frank for a period of one year while she underwent intensive psychotherapy.

These illustrations serve as common examples of the use and abuse of physical punishment in modern society. Physical punishment is frequently used as a means of behavior control and has a long history. Consider the following observations:

The physical punishment of children has a long well-substantiated history. For example, in the seventeenth century, the King of France instructed his son's mentor to whip the prince so he would become a better man. Flogging began when the royal child was just two years old. Several respected religious leaders, among them John Calvin, preached that parents' duty to God and to the child required breaking the will of the infant at the earliest possible age. That this dictum was taken seriously is shown in a parents' magazine published in the early nineteenth century. One young mother wrote a righteous account of whipping her 16-month-old daughter until the child would repeat the phrase "Dear Momma" on demand. (Elizabeth Elmer, "Child Abuse and Family Stress," *Journal of Social Issues*, 1979, 35, p. 64).

History shows that for centuries youth have had no rights, and maltreatment was socially sanctioned in order to discipline and educate. In Roman times the Patria Potestas allowed the father to sell, sacrifice, mutilate, or kill his offspring. The parents, educators, and ministers of Colonial America were influenced by biblical injunctions from Proverbs such as:

> *He who spares his rod hates his son, but he who loves him disciplines him diligently.* (Proverbs 13:24)
> *Do not hold back discipline from the child; although you beat him with the rod, he will not die.*
> *You shall beat him with the rod, and deliver his soul from Sheol.* (Proverbs 23:13-14)

(Rodger W. Bybee, "Violence Toward Youth: A New Perspective," *Journal of Social Issues*, 1979, 35, p. 2).

Such statements point out the historical and cultural antecedents for the present emphasis on the use of physical punishment. Translations of Proverbs tend to equate physical punishment with discipline. It is alarming that these dicta have sanctioned the use of physical punishment for infants. Elizabeth Elmer cites evidence that physical punishment in infant management is a practice of some mothers.

It is somewhat shocking, nevertheless, to find that some parents even hit babies a month or two old. Korsch and her colleagues interviewed 100 mothers of infants, who were out-patients in Los Angeles clinics. The investigation defined any kind of physical punishment as spanking. *One-quarter* of the mothers had started to mete out this type of punishment before their babies were six months of age. Almost *half* the women were spanking infants under twelve months of age, even though they believed it was better to defer such punishment until the age of one year. (Elizabeth Elmer, "Child Abuse and Family Stress," *Journal of Social Issues,* 1979, 35, p. 64).

The suggestion that physical punishment of infants is a common practice is shocking because of the increased risk of child abuse. It is known that victims of child abuse are from families that rely on punitive discipline. Lamentably, spanking is often allowed to escalate into beatings and other more pernicious forms of violence. Infants are physically vulnerable to even the mildest forms of physical violence; hence physical punishment frequently results in injury to the child. That this so often occurs is a primary reason for my unwillingness to prescribe spanking as a useful management technique.

In a scientific sense, spanking is not a very effective method of extinguishing a particular behavior. A spanking usually temporarily suppresses the bad behavior but rarely eliminates it. Furthermore, the behavior is usually suppressed only in the presence of the punishing agent, and continues to occur when the punishing agent is not present. This is true because the motivation or reinforcement for the undesirable behavior continues to exist. Spanking may even *increase* the incentive for misbehavior because it is a form of attention and may have a reinforcing effect.

Many adults do not pause to consider the nature of the example that spanking sets for their children. From the most fundamental perspective, spanking is an attempt to control the behavior of a smaller person through physical aggression. The act of spanking inadvertently sanctions the use of physical aggression in an attempt to punish or change the behavior of another. Young children who are frequently spanked are apt to display aggressive acts when dissatisfied with the behavior of a peer. This tendency has been documented in the research literature concerning aggressive behavior in children. Theorists who hold extreme positions have maintained that the physical punishment of children provides the basis for war and all other forms of human aggression. Although this oversimplifies the explanation of human aggression, the statement is food for thought.

A final pitfall of spanking that I will mention pertains to the negative emotions that are created by the punishment. Consider for a moment how you might feel if someone much larger than yourself actually hit you. Your first reaction might be one of intense anger. You might act directly on that anger by hitting back or calling the police (hitting by a person who is not a family member legally constitutes an assault). You may choose to act more indirectly by anonymously attacking the aggressor. Such passive-aggressive acts tend to vary according to the relationship between the aggressor and the initial victim. A child may "forget" to pass on important messages to the adult, "lose" the car keys, or turn in failing work at school. After the anger fades, the child might feel sad and depressed that his dignity and human rights were violated. Finally, a general sense of fear, anxiety, or hostility might pervade future associations with other people in positions of authority. All the feelings that are elicited by hitting are negative and destructive and may lead to undesirable behavior. Although some adults contend that spanking produces a respect for authority, it is more likely that the opposite effect occurs.

EFFECTIVE USE OF PHYSICAL PUNISHMENT

Physical punishment acts to temporarily suppress a particular undesirable behavior. That can be quite useful if the child is involved in a dangerous activity. Playing with matches, hastily crossing the street, or manipulating sharp objects are examples of dangerous behaviors. A firm spanking coupled with explanations of the reasons for the spanking should suppress the behavior long enough to teach more appropriate responses to potentially dangerous situations. Statements such as "This hurts me more than it does you" or "I have to spank you because I love you" should be avoided. Such statements tend to reinforce the behavior and may sound insincere or phony to the child.

ALTERNATIVES
TO PHYSICAL PUNISHMENT

One of the most effective methods of eliminating an undesirable behavior is called *extinction*. The procedure simply involves the removal of reinforcers for a behavior. For example, we know that parental attention is a reinforcer for temper tantrums. Such episodes can be easily extinguished by ignoring the behavior. Hence the reinforcer (attention) is eliminated and the behavior (temper tantrums) ceases. Extinction can be effectively applied to a large number of bad behaviors, including crying, complaining, swearing, and so on. Adults will typically observe an increase in the intensity of the undesirable behavior soon after the reinforcer for that behavior is eliminated. This is a symptom of the child's frustration and should also be ignored. The effect is similar to that of putting coins in a soft-drink machine and not getting the drink. Most people will become frustrated and many will pound or kick the machine. Provided that the machine continues to "ignore" such behavior, the frustrated person will soon give up and walk away. Most undesirable behaviors demonstrated by children are not so intense that they pose threats of bodily harm or property damage; therefore, it is practical to ignore them.

A procedure called *time-out* should be used if the behavior is so intense that the child should be removed from the situation. Time-out, a variant of extinction, usually involves isolating the child immediately subsequent to episodes that are potentially destructive or physically hazardous. Fighting, throwing objects, or intense tantrums are behaviors that are effectively managed by time-out. The child should be immediately taken to a lighted and well-ventilated area and told to stay for a given length of time (usually one minute for each year of age). For example, a seven-year-old who is angry and throwing utensils in the kitchen could be escorted to the laundry room and told: "Time-out for throwing things. You will stay for seven minutes." Do not argue with the child or acknowledge any further bad behaviors. Avoid placing the child in a stimulating room where toys, music, or television are available which would actually reinforce the bad behavior. Finally, do not offer unusual attention or affection when the child is dismissed from time-out. Discuss your reasons for using time-out if the child inquires, but, again, do not get trapped into an argument. As you can see, the object of the extinction procedures is to give as little attention to the bad behavior as possible. Time-out is an extremely effective procedure when applied appropriately with physical punishment.

It is quite possible that an angry child may not comply with the time-out procedure. The probability of this event can be reduced by rehearsals. Also, beginning use of the procedure at an early age when children are easily removed from the situation and placed into time-out will reduce their subsequent tendency to refuse to comply with the procedure. However, children who refuse to comply with time-out should be isolated from all potentially reinforcing circumstances until they comply. Interaction with people, games, television, appetizing foods, and so forth, should be avoided. Most children will eventually conclude that a few minutes in time-out is a small price to pay for regaining access to all of the previously reinforcing events. Major reinforcers should be withheld until compliance is demonstrated.

One commonly used method of punishment is the withdrawal of privileges or rewards. Children are often "grounded," or not allowed to leave the house, as punishment. Other privileges, such as television, allowance, or swimming, may be revoked. Another example might involve two children who are fighting over the selection of television programs. The adult observes this conflict, walks over to the television and turns it off. In this example, fighting was punished by withdrawal of television, which is a privilege. The undesirable behavior is less likely to occur in the future.

CONCLUSION

Too much energy is wasted in an attempt to encourage children *not* to exhibit certain behaviors. Unnecessary emphasis and attention is given to the bad behavior. I contend that the best way to get a child to stop doing something is to replace the bad behavior with another, more desirable behavior. Remember that children are always behaving, and much of that behavior may be undesirable or bad. If such behavior is eliminated, another activity must supplant the bad behavior. Without careful thought and planning there is a reasonable chance that the new behavior will also be undesirable. Provided that parents discuss expectations and offer competent instruction as to how their expectations can be accomplished, much of the bad behavior will automatically be eliminated. Overall, it involves a positive approach with the emphasis on rewarding good behavior as opposed to punishing bad behavior. For example, fighting is best eliminated by means of instruction and reinforcement for cooperative play. Thus, if the children are cooperating, by definition they will not be fighting (unless, of course, the fight is construed as an athletic contest or another such cooperative endeavor). This type of positive approach to management is being successfully implemented in a large number of families today. The positive approach is in no way lenient or permissive. Precisely the

same goals are achieved as compared to a punitive approach—
however, in a more efficient and effective manner with fewer
adverse consequences.

seven

CONTRACTS
AND TOKEN
PROGRAMS

CASE EXAMPLE

Seventeen-year-old Terry was experiencing a great deal of conflict with her parents over the use of the family automobile on weekends. Terry reasoned that because she received good grades in school and made a special effort to help clean the house and do yard work on weekends, she should be allowed to have the car for recreational purposes. Her friends were able to stay out until 2:00 A.M., so Terry thought that her parents' curfew of 12:00 midnight was too restrictive and thus she ignored it. Terry's father responded to her late arrival with anger and threats to curtail any future use of the car. Weekend evenings often became occasions for prolonged arguments, with her father sometimes giving in and Terry making promises that she often did not keep. Terry's argument that she was a good student and did a lot for her parents compared to her friends was devalued by her father who responded with, "You eat and sleep here, don't you? We pay your tuition. Your grades had better be good!" The degree of conflict between Terry and her father often led to her mother's being asked by both parties to mediate the dispute. That only served to draw her into the middle of the fight and the mother soon avoided that role entirely.

The illustration represents a common occurrence between parents and children. Children often expect privileges based on one set of expectations and parents often have a different view of what their children can reasonably be expected to do. The failure to agree on "who gets what from whom for doing what" usually leads to restrictive, punitive attempts by both parties to control the other. An effective way of changing this type of situation lies in the use of contracts.

Contracts represent an agreement between two (or more) parties to exchange reinforcers, or desirable consequences. The main criterion that defines a workable contract is that both parties must agree to the terms. One often hears of "contracts" that are unilateral, or imposed by one person on another. They do not really represent an agreement because the unrepresented party usually tries to escape the terms of the contract, while the other party strives to enforce it. The two common uses of the term thus serve to underline the essential feature of mutuality that defines contracts as they are used in changing behavior. Both parties must be allowed to define the terms of the contract if effectiveness is really desired.

Contracts can be informal, as when two children agree to take turns sharing a toy, or quite elaborate, such as a couple's negotiating a written agreement covering finances, childrearing, housekeeping, and other matters. Most authors describe contracts as requiring five basic elements:

1. Each party clearly spells out what he/she will do.
2. The behaviors selected to be exchanged should be observable and thus able to be monitored by the parties.
3. Penalties for noncompliance should be included.
4. Bonus clauses should be included for exceptional or continued appropriate performance.
5. An accurate record of performance and delivery of agreed upon reinforcers should be kept and available for review.

The first consideration of clearly specifying the responsibilities of those involved is a pivotal element in any program of behavior change. The failure to completely specify what each party can expect to receive may encourage the "bait and switch" tactics used by unscrupulous sellers who claim to offer something but later try to extract a higher price or substitute an inferior product. A key element in negotiating any contract is the trust that each party has in the other to abide by the terms of the agreement. Most contracts take the form of a written agreement but contracts may also be negotiated between individuals who lack the required verbal skills. The main emphasis is on the agreement and its understanding, rather than on its technical, written form. An example involves a three-year-old boy who refused to brush his teeth despite parental explanations, encouragement, and threats. An agreement was made to link toothbrushing to receipt of toy adventure characters or Matchbox cars, and other items that previously had been given without any specified contingency. The boy was too young to read, so the contract used pictures to illustrate the behaviors to be exchanged, namely toothbrushing and toys. One snapshot showed the boy brushing his teeth; another showed him getting a toy from his smiling parents.

Another consideration involved in using contracts concerns monitoring compliance. The choice of using observable behaviors in negotiating the terms of a contract greatly facilitates monitoring. In the preceding example, both toothbrushing and receiving toys are easily observed and thus appropriate. In general, it is most effective to negotiate only that behavior for which an observable standard exists, such as doing chores or being home on time. Behaviors that are not readily observable, such as driving at the speed limit while alone, choosing friends, or refraining from sexual activity on dates, cannot be monitored accurately. It is not advisable to contract for such types of behaviors.

Penalties for noncompliance represent the third element often found in behavior contracts. This component is negotiated in advance along with other aspects of the contract and thus represents part of the overall agreement. The use of prescribed penalties helps prevent future conflict if one party fails to live up to the contract, and will provide compensation for the slighted party. Contracted use of penalties helps prevent the risk of having the entire agreement collapse. An individual is also prevented from taking unfair advantage of the other by arbitrarily changing the terms of the contract. Penalties often take the form of monetary compensation (that is, husband agrees to pay his wife $5.00 for each time he forgets to call home when he is going to be late).

A fourth element that can facilitate compliance with a contract is the use of bonus clauses. Bonuses are also determined in advance and are used to provide incentive for high levels of participation or appropriate compliance over long periods of time. For example, in the toothbrushing situation described previously, a bonus of a trip to the ice cream store was given for seven days of perfect performance, defined as brushing both morning and evening without being told. The criterion for compliance was brushing only six of the seven days each week. Thus, the bonus reflected high levels of participation. Bonus incentives may also serve to reinforce performance over long periods of time, such as the case of extending a child's curfew by one hour after a month of being home on time. Bonuses represent an excellent method of building extra motivation because they are specified in advance and are directly related to the goals of the contract.

The final consideration in discussions of contracts involves keeping adequate records of performance and delivery of rewards. Adequate records serve as a basis for evaluating performance and they encourage productive discussion concerning performance. Most participants are surprised to discover that much of the commentary is quite favorable.

A sample contract on the next page (Figure 5) represents a solution to the case presented in the beginning of the chapter. The wishes of each party are made explicit. Terry is allowed to be out an hour later on one night per week and she is told that her efforts at being a good daughter are appreciated. In return, she agrees to abide by the curfew rules and maintain her housework and academic performance at current levels. Terry's Dad negotiated a slightly later curfew on one night in return for Terry's accepting his desired curfew time on the other nights. He also extracted an agreement from Terry that she would lose her car privileges for the weekend if she is more than 15 minutes late. Both Terry and her father agreed to deal directly with each other and not get her mother involved. There is also a provision for a bonus based on exceptional behavior.

TOKEN PROGRAMS

A very effective means of reinforcing behavior is the use of tokens. Contracts may be seen as representing a type of barter system, where behaviors are exchanged. Token systems are more like our monetary system, in which money represents a symbol that is given at one time and is later used to purchase other items. Some type of tangible item, such as poker chips, tickets, or points, is used to reinforce behavior in a token system. The strength of tokens as reinforcers is based on the primary reinforcers that tokens are used to buy. The term *token economy* thus represents a situation analogous to our own economy, whereby money serves as the token used to acquire food, clothing, shelter, and recreation.

75

FIGURE 5

CONTRACT

Terry agrees to the following:

1. Be home by 11:00 P.M. on either Friday or Saturday night (must be stated before leaving).
2. Continue to help around the house and study as before.

Dad agrees to the following:

1. Allow Terry to use the car until 1:00 A.M. on one night of her choosing (must be stated before leaving) and 11:00 P.M. the other night.
2. Tell Terry he appreciates her grades and her help around the house.

Both parties agree to:

1. Discuss disagreements directly with each other and leave Mom out.

BONUS

1. Dad agrees to extend Terry's curfew to 2:00 A.M. and 12:00 midnight if she is home on time for four consecutive weekends and maintains on-time behavior at the new level thereafter.
2. Terry agrees to cook a special supper for Mom and Dad once per month while the contract is in effect.

REVIEW

Compliance with the contract will be reviewed each Sunday night after dinner. A written note of the discussion initialed by both parties will represent the record of the agreement.

Signatures:

                   ‾‾‾‾‾‾‾‾   ‾‾‾‾‾‾‾‾
                     Dad   *Terry*

Token programs can be divided into two types. The first type is called a *token system,* and usually focuses on one or two behaviors. A particular symbol (that is, stars on a chart, points written on a card) serves as the reinforcer for a particular behavior. An example is a system whereby a child would receive a check on a wall chart for being home on time from school, helping with dishes, and finishing homework. The checks would then allow the child to watch television for an extra hour each evening if desired. Token systems thus resemble contracts that use a symbol to reinforce behavior immediately and later allow access to a reinforcing event.

Token economies represent more complex types of token systems that generally cover a much broader range of behaviors and provide a much wider choice of rewards. Particular behaviors are reinforced with tokens. The available rewards are assigned prices that indicate how many tokens must be spent in order to get the valued item or privilege. Fines for bad behavior may be imposed and tokens may be saved and accumulated. However, an effort should be made to achieve a rough balance between earning and spending in order to keep motivation at the highest level.

Token economies are most successful in settings where a high degree of control is allowed over the available rewards. If children receive reinforcement without earning tokens, the balance of the economy is disturbed and little earning (and thus little desirable behavior) will occur. Therefore, token economies should be employed in camps, residential centers, institutions, and other highly structured settings; token systems are recommended for home use.

The use of token economies creates several difficult problems of implementation compared to other methods. The notion of an economy stresses accurate recording of earning and spending and requires fairly involved bookkeeping. The paper work is further increased when savings and fines for negative behavior are included in a program.

Token programs are not commonplace in our society, although they can be quite effective. Because tokens are not used everywhere, a need eventually arises to transfer token reinforcement to more naturally occurring rewards, such as approval or praise. Unfortunately, these naturally occurring rewards frequently do not maintain behavior. Thus, it is advisable to build in a token-free period at the end of a program.

eight

A LOOK
AT COMMON
BEHAVIOR
PROBLEMS

A wide range of behavior problems that parents and caretakers frequently observe in children is presented in this chapter. I attempt to discuss the causes and management strategies in a straightforward manner, as well as provide actual case examples and illustrations. Of course, the names and details of the case illustrations are altered to conceal identifying data.

AGGRESSIVE BEHAVIOR

Nine-year-old Karl was suspended from school because of his extremely aggressive behavior. He would indiscriminately throw punches at the children and destroy their books and school supplies, and he even assaulted an elderly librarian. The principal stated that Karl represented a physical threat to his classmates and school personnel; thus, he was removed from the school environment with a recommendation for immediate psychological counseling. The psychologist found that Karl has a reading disability that prevents him from performing on grade level academically. To make matters worse, Karl's father is an alcoholic who is prone toward explosive temper outbursts when intoxicated.

The case of Karl constitutes an extreme, but not uncommon, illustration of aggressive behavior. *Aggressive behavior* is a label or category that represents an extensive array of behaviors whose common result is the production of pain, discomfort, injury, or destruction of property. Common examples of aggressive behavior include hitting, pinching, yelling, pushing, and so forth. Aggression is usually a response to a frustrating or anger-evoking event. A child is often aggressive when he or she is denied a desirable object or participation in a desired activity. Aggression may occur as an act of retaliation in response to being the victim of aggression. As the child grows more sophisticated, aggression may become a means to an end and may occur independently of anger and frustration.

The ways that children learn to cope with anger and frustration largely depend on the models that are observed at home and at school. Children who observe hitting, yelling, or blaming at home are more likely to demonstrate such characteristics. Children who observe adults constructively attacking the problem (and not the people associated with it) are more likely to deal effectively with anger. The process involves the recognition and correct identification of anger and the subsequent appropriate expression of it. For example, a six-year-old who is not allowed to take home the fire truck that he sees on a shopping trip should be allowed to say, "I'm upset because I want that truck and you won't let me have it." Reasons should be given for denying the toy and a mutual plan devised as to how the child might eventually acquire the truck. That would be an appropriate expression and resolution of the angry feelings.

If appropriate expression of anger is not encouraged, more inappropriate expression (that is, aggression) will occur. There are several steps that should be taken whenever aggressive behavior is observed. First, ignore innocuous aggressive acts, such as verbal taunts or foot stamping. Offering no attention to such acts should extinguish them rather quickly. Time-out procedures should be applied to more destructive behavior that threatens property or physical harm. Isolating the child will serve to prevent further damage, allow for a cooling off period, and eliminate the possibility of incidental reinforcement. Under no circumstances should the child's aggression pay off by your relenting to his or her wishes.

Adults eventually learn to recognize situations that precipitate anger and aggression. An adult should learn to anticipate episodes and planfully encourage constructive responses to such situations. Children can learn to attack problems as vociferously as they attack people or objects.

Many adults discourage the direct expression of anger. That is unfortunate because their children will find indirect outlets for their hostility. Such behavior is euphemistically called passive-aggressive. Consider the following example:

Judy became quite upset when she was told that her classmate, Paula, would not be allowed to spend the night on Friday. Judy was scolded upon showing her anger and told to be quiet. That night Judy "accidentally" spilled a glass of grape juice on the new sofa in the den.

Judy's spilling the grape juice was a passive-aggressive expression of her anger and frustration. Perhaps the unfortunate event might have been avoided had her feelings been previously resolved.

Once aggressive behavior develops as an enduring trend, it may become detached from anger. Violent acts are then calculated and planned events that are employed to accomplish some specific goal. Examples of such behavior might include rape, armed robbery, or premeditated murder.

At that point, aggressive behavior has become a well-established personality trait that requires long-term professional intervention with no guarantee of success. Therefore, appropriate management of aggression in early childhood is stressed.

BED WETTING *Imipromine (Tofranol)*

Harold is a seven-year-old and has been free from bed wetting incidents for approximately four years. However, Harold's maternal grandmother died of cancer six months ago, which precipitated frequent episodes of nighttime wetting. It became a matter of great concern to Harold and he grew increasingly ashamed and embarrassed about his problem. Harold's mother consulted the family pediatrician, who recommended a simple management program for Harold, resulting in immediate resolution of the problem.

Enuresis is the term for day- or nighttime wetting past the age of four. Involuntary wetting must occur once a month or more to be considered a behavioral problem. Most children will have occasional accidents when excited, in a new environment, or subsequent to drinking large amounts of liquids. Bed wetting is considered to be more an annoyance than an indication of a serious behavioral or emotional problem. Parents and caretakers expend a great deal of effort in changing bedclothes and pajamas. As childen grow older, bed wetting creates embarrassment and often stigmatizes them. Obviously, bed wetting is an undesirable problem and one that is treatable.

After determining that bed wetting has reached problem status, a pediatrician or family doctor should be consulted to rule out the possibility of medical involvement. In most cases enuresis does not have a physical component; once that is clear, the parents should proceed with a behavioral strategy. The first step is to disallow any ingestion of liquids for approximately three hours prior to bedtime. Make sure that the child has had plenty to drink before the three-hour period. The child should be required to urinate immediately before going to bed. Subsequently, an alarm should be set for 2:00 or 3:00 A.M. and placed close to a door that leads to the bathroom. The child should learn how to use the alarm clock and should be responsible for turning it off in the middle of the night. The child's parents should get up during the first three or four nights to make sure that the child gets up, turns off the alarm, and uses the toilet for urination. Dry sheets in the morning should be recognized by rewarding the child with a star or other token that can be exchanged for something of value. This exchange should not occur until the child has established a pattern of improved performance. Significant improvement is usually observed within a week or two. Accidents and setbacks should be ignored because punishment or ridicule usually produces undesirable consequences.

My experience shows that the foregoing plan should result in significant improvement of the problem within a month to six weeks. If the child continues to wet the bed, the parents should consider a moisture-sensitive bed pad that is connected to a buzzer, an effective conditioning procedure whereby the tension of a full bladder gradually replaces the buzzer as a cue to awaken and urinate. Such devices are available in many mail-order houses and some drugstores. Most family doctors will know where they can be purchased.

If none of the above procedures proves useful, in-depth medical and psychological intervention may be required. Some physicians prescribe medication and recommend psychotherapy with psychologists or psychiatrists. Such steps should be taken only after the above strategies have been conscientiously implemented. Remember that bed wetting is not bad and the child should in no way be blamed for its occurrence. Bed wetting may be eliminated by simply ignoring it; however, the above suggestions can be applied when you feel ready.

NONCOMPLIANCE

Jerry is a seventh grader at Rosewood Junior High School. He was referred to the Child Development Clinic because of his refusal to obey common requests by his parents, teachers, and others in authority. His parents stated: "Sometimes we think that he doesn't even hear us. For example, we often call him to supper while he is absorbed in a television program. He will not budge, so we have to walk into the den and turn the television off before he hears our instructions. When we ask him to mow the grass or run incidental errands for us he never seems to get around to finishing the job. Jerry's not a bad kid. We just want to find out if something is mentally or physically wrong with him." Subsequent to a complete team evaluation, the Child Development Clinic staff proposed a token strategy to motivate Jerry to comply with the requests of his parents and teachers.

Noncompliance is a general category of behaviors denoting the child's refusal to obey the requests of an adult. Many parents complain about their child's disobedience regarding listening to and completing various assignments. Parents often ask children to take out the garbage, clean their rooms, pick up toys, or do their homework only to discover later that the tasks have not been done. Adults must create an environment that provides adequate motivation for getting the job done.

Perhaps the most common consequence of noncompliance is nagging and fussing. How often do we hear comments such as, "Bobby, I have asked you to take the garbage out three times and this time I mean it." Bobby has every reason to believe that his father did not really "mean it" before. Furthermore, such nagging focuses a great deal of attention on the undesirable behavior (that is, not taking out the garbage). As discussed, it may serve to inadvertently reinforce the undesirable behavior.

A much more effective strategy involves the provision of attention and reward when Bobby returns from taking out the garbage. Simply saying "Thank you for the excellent job" is a powerful reward. You may also agree to making dessert or allowing television time contingent on taking the garbage out; that is, Bobby is denied dessert and the privilege of watching television until the chore has been completed. The activity would become so routine that the parent would not have to remind the child to finish the task.

WITHDRAWN BEHAVIOR

Four-year-old Helen was always described as a timid, shy, and reticent child, who preferred solitary play to engaging in group play activities. She was frightened by strangers, particularly men, and grew tearful when faced with most novel situations or events. Helen's parents had read that playing with peers was an important aspect of child development; therefore, they were concerned about her tendency to withdraw from most social situations. Several adults in the neighborhood suggested that Helen's parents contact a certain preschool teacher who was particularly sensitive to the needs of extremely shy children. Because of the skill and sensitivity on the part of the teacher, Helen was gradually drawn out of her shell.

Some children are friendly and outgoing, whereas others are reserved and introverted. There is a wide range of acceptable behaviors along the introversion—extroversion continuum. Many quiet and shy children are viewed favorably, particularly by teachers who often expend considerable energy in attempting to suppress their more rowdy peers. However, many children fail to establish satisfying relationships because of their tendency to withdraw. Such children usually spend a great deal of time in solitary play and will actively avoid overtures to become involved in activities. Many possible causes for such behavior exist; however, it will be more helpful to work with the symptoms as opposed to probing the causes of extreme withdrawn behavior.

The *shaping* procedure is the desired approach for training children to make cooperative, interpersonal responses. A specific goal, such as "amount of time spent in cooperative play," should be established. Successive approximations to achieving that goal should be rewarded. The adult should initially praise and reward fundamental interpersonal responses, such as appropriate eye contact and simple verbalizations. Merely sitting in a group may be a positive step for a withdrawn child. Once simple behaviors have been established, more complex interactive behavior is trained. Such behaviors might include sharing a box of raisins, participating in a game that requires cooperation, or discussing the experience of a field trip.

The adult should not apply too much pressure to interact because the child will only grow more withdrawn. Steps toward the goal should be very gradual and progress will likely temporarily halt or reverse throughout the course of training for appropriate social behavior. The adult should attempt to ensure that all of the child's interactions are pleasant and rewarding rather than aversive or punitive. It is often helpful to involve the child's peers in the program so that they are praised and rewarded for interacting in a pleasant manner with the withdrawn child. That must be handled with some delicacy to prevent the children from overacting, which only exacerbates the withdrawn behavior.

Shy, withdrawn children will frequently respond with nonverbal social gestures, such as a nod, a certain grimace or look, or a particular body posture. Adults should be especially sensitive to such cues offered by the withdrawn child. Correct interpretation of messages often builds trust and rapport that later prove helpful in encouraging the child to interact.

DISHONESTY

Rebecca is a ten-year-old who has recently been engaged in a number of incidents that involve lying. The school social worker made a home visit to interview the parents concerning Rebecca's bothersome problem. On arriving at Rebecca's home, the social worker noticed a radar detection device on the dashboard of the family car. The phone rang during the interview and Rebecca's mother directed the child to answer the phone and tell the party that no one else was home. Rebecca's mother greatly exaggerated many of the routine facts that were requested for the file. She revealed that Rebecca's father was in legal trouble for income tax evasion. As the interview progressed, the social worker became acutely aware that Rebecca's home was a fertile breeding ground for dishonest behavior.

Most adults place considerable value on teaching children to be truthful. Honesty is a basic principle that many people believe should underlie all interpersonal exchanges to ensure a harmoniously functioning society. Unfortunately, many children learn that telling the truth does not always pay off in practical terms. It is helpful to take a closer look at the process.

Children quickly learn that honest and candid comments frequently result in unpleasant consequences. Consider the first-grader who tells his father's boss that he has bad breath. Shock, embarrassment, and anxiety are emotions that dominate most similar situations. The child will likely be subjected to a lengthy lecture on the value of discretion and the necessity of not offending people, regardless of the cost. Children learn to keep quiet and to develop a fabric of "white lies" that facilitates social acceptability. From that point, it is a small step to rationalizing or justifying falsehoods of a more serious nature.

Children are frequently punished for telling the truth about a previous misdeed. In that case, the punishment will have more of a suppressive effect on truthful behavior than on the deed in question. Punishment is effective in decreasing behavior only when applied immediately following the behavior; therefore, truth-telling is suppressed because it is the most recent link in the chain of behaviors. The child then learns to avoid punishment by telling lies.

Young children do not have the intellectual or cognitive

ability always to distinguish reality from fantasy. Frequently they create imaginative tales that are based in fantasy. Fantasy is also encouraged in children's literature and folklore—from Pinocchio to Santa Claus. Children are then immersed in a world that has little or no basis in reality or truth. Fantasy activity serves many useful purposes; however, it should always be distinguished from reality. The tales should be couched in terms of a game that is to be enjoyed rather than portrayed as truth in literal terms. Many adults react strongly to reducing the status of the tooth fairy and Santa Claus to fantasy figures. People often contend that they are essential ingredients of a full and happy childhood experience. My response is basically threefold. First, children are able to enjoy participating in such games even though the activities are structured as pretending exercises. For example, the child who enjoys "playing soldier" is usually never told that he *is* a soldier. The child will be enchanted when you say, "let's pretend that the tooth fairy is coming tonight." Furthermore, children can experience the same amount of enthusiasm and excitement in the face of natural events. A trip to the zoo can easily match the excitement engendered by visions of Santa Claus, provided that the accompanying adults share in the enthusiasm. Finally, children who are led to believe in the myths of our culture are technically reared in a web of falsehoods. They are often disillusioned in response to learning that their favorite figures do not exist in reality. One possible effect is that the child may become more skeptical of adult points of view regarding a variety of more important issues. Hence the child may reject the adult's attitudes concerning ethics, religion, and personal values—the adult has lost credibility.

Adults must take a hard, objective look at the examples they set. It is helpful to ponder and discuss views about honesty and whether or not absolute honesty is a goal to be achieved. Many adults consciously decide that the use of lies or "white lies" is morally acceptable. Do you make critical and disparaging remarks about people, but behave in a conciliatory manner in their presence? Do you make excuses for not engaging in certain activities? Do you consciously disobey various laws and actively avoid getting caught? If the answers to the questions are "Yes," then you can expect to see similar behavior in your children. That may or may not be undesirable from your perspective.

SIBLING CONFLICT

Shirley and Diane are fraternal twins. From the earliest age, they were referred to as "the twins" and encouraged to participate in the same activities. In many ways they were treated as one individual and began to compete for attention and recognition. They grew possessive of their belongings and each drew imaginary boundaries in their bedroom that the other was not allowed to penetrate. Shirley and Diane became openly hostile toward each other and required close supervision to prevent vociferous arguments and occasional fighting. The tension grew intolerable to the point that their parents consulted a family counselor to create a plan that would eliminate the hostility between the two.

Sibling rivalry is a common childhood problem that is largely preventable and can be treated if allowed to occur. Although this discussion is focused on sibling rivalry, the suggestions may also be applied to relationships among children outside the family.

The term *rivalry* connotes an intense competitive relationship between two or more individuals. Siblings compete for parental attention and praise, as well as for other resources available in the family system. This rivalrous relationship can be prevented by adequately preparing the older sibling for the arrival of the newborn. Older children should be encouraged to participate in various activities that pave the way for a new member of the family, such as toy selection or arranging the nursery. Once the newborn is home, older siblings should help with child care so that tending to the infant's needs becomes a responsibility that is shared by the entire family. Friends who visit the family of the newborn should take a favor or memento to other siblings when a gift is presented to the baby. People should, at the very least, be careful not to ignore the other children. Parents should also set aside routine periods solely devoted to the older siblings to satisfy their need for individual attention. As the children grow older, it is advisable to avoid unnecessary comparisons, such as "Johnny is better looking than Mike, but Mike is the better student."

Adults must encourage cooperation and discourage competition once a problem has been detected. This can best be achieved through creating jobs or tasks in which the siblings are required to work together to achieve a common goal. A certain amount of creativity is called for to discover activities that require siblings to work as a team. However, this can often occur in the natural environment, particularly when siblings have to unite to protect themselves against some outside threat, such as a neighborhood bully. Such a situation may facilitate considerable cohesion among siblings provided that they act as a unit to protect each other.

Competition among siblings can be reduced if the children are allowed to choose separate activities based on interests and abilities. One child may be interested in athletics, while the other could be interested in art. Siblings should be encouraged to make independent decisions concerning their use of free time. Parents may consider placing their children on separate teams or in separate classes if the siblings express similar interests.

Attempts to coerce close bonds or friendships among siblings usually prove useless. Although conflict and rivalry can be reduced, children cannot be forced to establish close friendships with others. However, close ties are encouraged by not applying pressure to be friends, avoiding comparisons, and allowing siblings to grow as individuals.

MASTURBATION

Amy's mother was distressed to discover her eight-year-old daughter massaging her genitals while lying in bed one morning. She felt that it was a repulsive and disgusting act, which constituted poor moral development and was physically unhealthy. However, she was reassured after talking with a pastoral counselor, who told her that exploring the genitals is a common and natural form of sexual expression among children. She was educated about the signals of excessive preoccupation with masturbation, as opposed to expressions of natural and healthy curiosity.

At some point between the ages of nine months and two years, most children will show interest in exploring and manipulating their genitals. Such behavior is most likely to occur during diapering or bathing, yet masturbation is by no means restricted to those settings. Masturbatory behavior is observed at varying rates throughout childhood, depending on age, sex, and individual differences. The point to remember is that manipulation of the genitals is a common phenomenon of childhood and does not reflect emotional or mental disturbance.

Adults should accept such behavior as a natural expression of curiosity. Of course, parents are concerned that the behavior occurs in appropriate private situations, which may require a bit of discrimination training. Parents shold calmly correct inappropriate masturbatory behavior by saying "No" or removing the child from the situation, if necessary. Most children quickly take the hint and discontinue the activity in the presence of others.

Excessive masturbation in children is clearly suggestive of underlying emotional difficulties that are usually associated with high levels of anxiety. The point at which the behavior is considered excessive may be difficult to specify; however, if you suspect that the child escapes responsibilities and copes with stress through masturbation, then the activity is excessive. Counseling or psychotherapy is recommended in order to identify and alleviate the stressors in the child's environment.

A prudent course of action is to consult a urologist to rule out the possibility of a urinary tract infection that may produce itching or burning. Children often appear to be engaged in masturbatory behavior in their attempt to relieve discomfort associated with infection. Tight-fitting clothing and strong detergents can also serve as irritants capable of producing similar discomfort. Such possibilities should also be investigated.

FEAR

> Jason is a fifth grader who sneaked into the television room and watched a late night murder mystery on the sly. The show was recommended for adults and was thought to be too terrifying for young children to watch. The murder took place in the upstairs of an old house after a frightening scene showing the murderer stalking the victim through a long corridor and up a narrow stairwell. Jason was so frightened by the stalking scene that he refused to enter hallways or staircases thereafter. Only after skilled intervention on the part of his parents did Jason overcome his fear.

Most people are familiar with an experiment performed by Russian scientist Ivan Pavlov, in which a dog was trained to salivate in response to a bell. The sound of the bell was associated with the presentation of food by sounding the bell just prior to presenting the food. Subsequent to several trials, Pavlov found that a dog would salivate in response to the sound of the bell alone. Pavlov's experiment had enormous impact on the study of human learning and behavior.

Further study has shown that such *classical conditioning* is the basis for learning many different emotions, including fear. Classical conditioning involves reflexive activity on the part of the organ systems that produce emotions. The organs of the endocrine system, as well as the smooth muscles, engender emotional response that prepares people to engage in such behavior as fighting, fleeing from a dangerous situation, or participating in reproductive activity. The cues that signal such behaviors are learned and vary widely among individuals. Thus the cues or stimuli that signal danger for African bush natives are vastly different from the fear-producing stimuli for Manhattan residents. Learning effective responses to unique fear-producing stimuli facilitates survival and adaptation to a particular environment. Yet there are many instances in which children learn to respond to nonthreatening situations with intense and immobilizing fear. Such fear is not adaptive and may actually interfere with vital development processes, as when the child develops school phobia.

Several natural or unconditioned stimuli for fear are observable in infants. Sudden loud noises, falling sensations, and pain generate endocrine responses that are interpreted by adults as fear. Such stimuli can become associated with any number of previously neutral cues, such that they become learned or conditioned stimuli for fear. In that way, a child may learn to fear strangers, dark clouds, shoes, television sets, flashing blue lights, or any other object or event in the environment. The stimuli can be paired with cues that are even further removed from the original fear-producing stimulus, thus creating multiple, irrational fears. Such fears are irrational in the sense that the stimuli pose no real threat of harm to the child. Unfortunately, many adults inadvertently encourage the fears by allowing children to avoid the fear-producing situations. Some adults control children's behavior by encouraging and exploiting irrational fears, for example, by saying, "the boogeyman will get you if you don't straighten up your room."

There are several techniques that, when used in combination, are entirely effective in the elimination of irrational fear. One such technique is a simple extinction procedure. I have said that an irrational fear is one that is learned and occurs in the face of a stimulus or situation that poses no real threat to the child. Repeated exposure to the harmless situation will eventually eliminate the fear. However, the fear may be sufficiently extreme even to prevent approaching the child with the stimulus. The child may scream, cry hysterically, and display other negative reactions. A more gradual approach is suggested for such intense fear.

Dr. Joseph Wolfe developed a technique, called *systematic desensitization,* that is quite effective in reducing intense fear. The technique was initially developed with adults but has recently been successfully adapted for use with children. A child is taught methods of relaxation utilizing deep breathing and muscle relaxation exercises. Learning to relax is essential because relaxation cannot occur simultaneously with fear. Once the child has learned to relax, fear-evoking images are presented in the order of least frightening to most frightening stimuli. Eventually the child learns to relax in response to the original fear-producing stimuli.

Younger children who are not as verbally adept must learn other ways to relax when confronted with fear-producing stimuli. Psychologists know that people cannot eat when intensely afraid; therefore, eating is incompatible with extreme fear. A child must be reasonably relaxed to eat. Given such information, a fear-producing stimulus can be gradually presented to the child when eating, in such a manner that the fear response is not allowed to develop. Gradual presentation of the stimulus might involve displaying the object or event at a distance and slowly approaching the child with it. The stimulus should be withdrawn if the child becomes uncomfortable. Fear-producing stimuli can also be gradually introduced by presenting items that are similar to the aversive stimulus. For example, children who are afraid of large dogs could be allowed to play with kittens, then puppies, and finally larger friendly dogs.

Strategies for eliminating irrational fears have been briefly introduced to enable the adult to manage mild fears effectively. A mental health professional should be consulted in the event of intense and enduring phobia. Such professonals are best equipped to treat emotionally damaging conditions.

SCHOOL REFUSAL

Mark refused to get out of the car at school to attend the first day of kindergarten. His parents were anxious for all to go well with his first school experience so they allowed him to return home to calm down. He was quite upset, as indicated by his outbursts of screaming and crying. The next day Mark awoke with an episode of nausea and stomach cramps. He was taken immediately to the pediatrician, who quickly diagnosed the problem as school refusal. A specific strategy for intervention was discussed with his parents, as well as with the school officials.

Most children are apprehensive about attending school for the first time and usually show mild anxiety and nervousness. However, they attend school and find the experience in general to be rewarding. A small minority of children display extreme anxiety, which is usually accompanied by such physical complaints as headache, stomach cramps, drowsiness, and nausea. When extreme fearfulness can be avoided only by not attending school, a school phobia has developed. These feelings may be evoked by the child's anxiety concerning separating from parents or it may be a response to an aversive condition at school.

The child should be referred to a specialist within three or four days of the onset of the problem. It is always advisable to consult a physician to rule out a medical problem that may be the basis for a child's physical and emotional problems. The child is usually referred to a psychologist or mental health professional, once he or she is deemed physically healthy. The psychologist typically suggests a combination of approaches that include fading, shaping, and extinction of anxiety. Parents may be "faded" out of the picture by having them accompany the child to the classroom and linger in the hall while their child adjusts to the classroom situation. Parents should not enter the classroom nor should they allow their child to escape the classroom. Attempts to avoid the classroom should be handled in a firm and direct, yet gentle, manner. Discussion of the problem in the presence of the child is discouraged. Shaping may be employed by gradually increasing the amount of time the child spends at school each day. Intervals of attendance can be increased by thirty minutes each day until the child is attending the full day. It is usually recommended that a child begin spending the time at the end of the day and work toward arriving earlier each day. In that way, the child quickly learns the appropriate cues for leaving school and is allowed to depart with peers. Finally, parents must withdraw rewards that are present at home when the child is not attending. Such rewards may include television, parental attention, and special outings. Such rewards should be contingent on school attendance.

School phobias may be prevented through careful planning and sensitivity to the child's concerns. It is frequently helpful to arrange a visit to the school prior to the first day of class. Orientation to the facility and introduction to the principal and teacher usually reduce apprehension and fear. School and education in general should be discussed in a positive light. Finally, potential concerns and fears should be recognized but not dwelled upon.

ANXIETY

Jimmy was always seen as a nervous child. He was a nail-biter and frequently bit his fingers until they bled. He had difficulty paying attention for any length of time and was extremely restless and fidgety. His breathing was often shallow and rapid and he complained of frequent head and stomach aches. His father demanded perfection of him in the classroom, in sports, and at home. Jimmy's father would often practice baseball with him and tended to react harshly to flaws in his performance. Jimmy was frequently compared, in an unfavorable light, to his older brother. He gradually developed an extreme condition of anxiety, which impaired his performance in many crucial areas of development.

Anxiety can be viewed as an emotional response that is similar to fear, but has a more general cause. In other words, anxiety is a nonspecific fear that can be encouraged by punitive discipline, excessive pressure to achieve, or other threatening circumstances.

Moderate levels of anxiety facilitate optimal performance in academics, athletics, and other areas of activity. Mild nervousness energizes children to put forth their best efforts in accomplishing various tasks. The anxiety diminishes once the goal has been attained and a sense of relaxation and satisfaction results. However, enduring levels of extreme anxiety are deleterious to the child's emotional and physical well-being. The child with severe anxiety experiences extreme emotional discomfort accompanied by fast heart rate, shallow breathing, sweaty palms, and increased physical activity. More stomach acid is produced than is normal, resulting in loose stools and stomach aches. Anxiety may create or compound respiratory problems and is associated with frequent and intense headaches.

Extreme anxiety can be prevented by employing positive, nurturing methods of discipline that minimize threat. Also, it is important to expect levels of performance that are commensurate with a child's ability. Expecting and demanding too much create tremendous pressure that is converted into anxious feelings. Exposing children to marital turmoil in the forms of yelling, hitting, or threats of separation also generates extreme anxiety.

Once anxiety has reached extreme levels, several approaches to intervention are usually recommended by the psychologist. Family counseling that focuses on pinpointing and eliminating sources of stress is often an effective strategy. For example, counseling may reveal that a child is concerned about the financial problems of the family. One solution would be to discontinue emotionally laden discussions about money in the presence of the child. The child may also be trained to physically relax through deep breathing and muscle tension exercises. Like fear, anxiety cannot coexist in a relaxed body. In extreme cases, medication may be recommended.

NIGHTMARES

> Bobby is an eleven-year-old who has been experiencing frequent nightmares over the past three months. He reports a recurrent dream that his family is killed in an automobile accident. Bobby wakes up screaming with sweat dripping from his face. He is unable to resume sleeping and demands that one of his parents sit up with him for the rest of the night. Interestingly, Bobby was informed by a friend at school that he was adopted, whereas his sister was his parents' "real" child. Bobby was told about the adoption just prior to the onset of the nightmares.

Nightmares are frightening dreams that are accompanied by acute anxiety, feelings of helplessness, and often a suffocating sensation. Virtually all children experience occasional nightmares because such dreams are often reflective of daytime anxieties. Frequent and persistent nightmares usually suggest inordinate amounts of stress. Obvious stressors, such as the loss of a relative or pet, divorce, illness, injury, or a new sibling, may precipitate nightmares. Additionally, subtle stressors also exist and may be beyond the child's or family's awareness.

The management of nightmares is particularly delicate because comforting the child may also serve as reinforcement of the problem. Frequent and persistent nightmares should be managed professionally. First, medical problems, such as irregular thyroid functioning or neurological impairment, should be investigated. Subsequently, investigation into family dynamics, as well as the child's emotional status, will dictate further intervention.

OBESITY:
A PREVENTIVE APPROACH

Obesity is the leading nutritional disorder in developed nations today. Although estimates vary, literally millions of Americans are plagued with the problem of obesity. Many individuals are dependable consumers of the endless array of fad diets, exercise and diet books, and other popular guides to weight control. The seeds of obesity are usually planted during infancy and early childhood. Prevention of adult eating problems is best achieved by means of a sensible approach to childhood nutrition.

Obesity has persisted throughout the recorded history of man. The pervasive problem knows no cultural or national boundaries. Further, the incidence of obesity has increased dramatically in recent history. Experts attribute the increase to a number of factors that have emerged from modern technology. Large amounts of highly caloric foods are more available to individuals in modern society than ever before. This is a result of startling increases in food production that were observed with the advent of sophisticated industrial technology. Hence greater quantities of food of a higher biologic quality have been catapulted into the American diet. Technology has also spurred the growth of a ubiquitous convenience or "fast food" industry that imposes even more calories on consumers. Other conveniences have contributed to a decline in individual energy expenditure. Automobiles, dishwashers, washers and dryers, and escalators are examples of common devices that discourage exercise. The pattern of increased caloric intake and decreased energy exertion is, lamentably, encroaching on the lifestyles of children.

The excess energy, or positive energy balance, is readily converted to fat. The fat, or adipose tissue, is stored for future energy requirements and is essential to normal human functioning. However, when excess fat accumulates by way of the positive energy balance, obesity occurs. The precise point at which an individual is considered obese is arbitrarily defined and measured by a variety of techniques. A cursory examination of the unclothed child will usually result in a valid conclusion.

The problems of obese individuals are numerous and tend to have considerable emotional impact. An obvious problem of obesity stems from its social consequences. Society often stigmatizes obese individuals by attributing undesirable traits to them. Overweight people are often thought to be lazy, messy, and lacking willpower. Obese people are frequently regarded as less attractive than their thinner peers. Physical activity can be significantly restricted for obese people, thus limiting their range of satisfying activities. Health hazards, particularly of a cardiovascular nature, may be found among overweight individuals. Finally, a poor self-concept and a predominant sense of helplessness are often associated with obesity.

Throughout infancy and early childhood the responsibility for children's nutrition lies primarily with parents. Some decisions concerning nutrition are usually made before a baby arrives. Most expectant parents contemplate such issues as the pros and cons of breastfeeding, feeding schedules, and when to introduce solid foods. Such decisions are critical for establishing optimally healthy feeding patterns early in life.

It is usually advisable to breastfeed the infant, if at all possible. There are several distinct advantages to breastfeeding. First, there are chemicals in mother's milk that produce immunity to a number of infections that could affect the infant. Second, the risk of impurities, usually in the form of bacteria, is eliminated by breastfeeding. Third, the emotional bonding process is facilitated by the comfort and satisfaction experienced by both mother and child. Finally, some mothers enjoy saving the money and effort involved in purchasing and preparing commercial formulas.

Disadvantages to breastfeeding should also be carefully examined. Mothers who nurse their infants must be continuously accessible to the child. Breastfeeding obviously precludes working or traveling in the child's absence. In many situations a marked social sanction against breastfeeding exists. (I recall an incident in which a mother was arrested for indecent exposure while nursing her infant in a public park.) This may serve to produce significant anxiety and discomfort for the mother, which sets a tone that is incompatible with emotional and physical nurturing. Finally, not every mother is capable of producing adequate supplies of milk. A mother may become needlessly frustrated or even feel guilty, at which point attempts to breastfeed should be suspended.

Commercial formulas are designed to simulate human milk in flavor and nutritional value. Formulas generally consist of a mixture of cow's milk, water, and sugar. Infants who are allergic to cow's milk are given powdered milk or goat's milk with other nutritional supplements.

Regardless of the particular type of food selected, parents should avoid all struggles in attempting to coerce a child to eat. Infants and children display a remarkable ability to regulate the amount of food required for optimal growth. Attempts to force the child to eat result in an increased resistance and rebelliousness at mealtime. Feeding can quickly turn into a dreaded activity characterized by tension and frustration. Parents should learn to recognize cues, such as distinctive crying or hand sucking, that signal the child's hunger. An infant is then receptive to food and will discontinue when satiated. Hence there is no specific quantity that the child should be expected to ingest at mealtime. Simply stated, infants accept food when hungry and reject it when satiated.

Controlled weight gain is the best indicator of appropriate nutrition. Although most infants lose several ounces in the two or three days following birth, weight gain should be continuous and gradual thereafter. There is considerable variability in the rate of weight gain; however, a rule of thumb is that birth weight should double by five to six months and increase about one pound per month until age one. The pediatrician should keep records of a child's weight—weighings outside of the doctor's office are unnecessary during the first year.

Unfortunately, many parents have erroneously been made to believe that fat infants are the result of superior care. Chubby babies have been portrayed as deliriously happy and healthy. The infant's physique is one of the few readily observable indices of parental care. Overfeeding is also encouraged by the fact that it is one of the few methods (other than holding, talking, and cleaning) of nurturing the child. Parents frequently offer food to the satiated, fussy baby to relieve anxiety in themselves. Such mistaken perceptions may result in a permanent addition of unnecessary fat cells.

Many parents are anxious to start infants on solid foods as early as possible because of their concern about weight gain. Most children are started on solid foods between two and four months, the specific time varying with the child. A child may begin to demand more feedings and an increase in the volume of milk at each feeding. The pediatrician or family doctor should advise the parent concerning the introduction of solid foods. However, it is important to note that solid foods should not be administered until the child shows clear evidence that he or she is physically ready. Scientific evidence supports the view that early administration of solid foods may result in obesity in later life. Although not true for all children, delaying the ingestion of solid foods certainly decreases the risk of obesity.

Solid foods are usually introduced in the following order: cereals, fruits, vegetables, and meats. A week or two between the introduction of each food group should be allowed. Foods are sold in pureed or strained form and the ingredients are noted on the container. Parents should generally avoid baby foods that have added sugar or starch. Vegetables mixed with refined grains (rice, corn, and wheat) or other starches should also be avoided. Fruits should be given for desserts in lieu of cakes, puddings, or other sweets.

Children should be allowed ample freedom in selecting the specific foods within the appropriate array of choices that parents offer. Given the freedom to choose, most children will naturally select the foods that are physically required at the time. Interestingly, studies show that children not only regulate the amounts of food required, but also the kinds of food required to achieve a balanced diet. This holds true particularly when the child is given ample freedom in selecting food and when unnecessary battles over food are avoided. In one study, children were deprived of certain specific nutrients for a few days. They were subsequently allowed to choose from a variety of foods displayed in a cafeteria. The children invariably selected foods that were rich in the substances previously withdrawn from their diets. Similar results have been observed in animals that were deprived of certain vitamins. The vitamin-deficient rats showed strong preferences for foods that were rich in the vitamins withheld. The data often contradict the intuitive thinking of adults. Many adults perceive children as naturally voracious consumers of cookies, cakes, ice cream, and candy, and as adamant opponents of fruits and vegetables. Such inappropriate food preferences are learned by subtle and intricate conditioning processes (see Chapter four) and do not represent the natural choices of the child.

Parents should provide a reasonable array of foods for selection. Ample choices of foods from each food group should be available. Children should be consulted about food preferences before embarking on a trip to the grocery store. It is recommended that parents avoid buying impulse items and purchase only the items specified on a carefully prepared grocery list. Such a procedure usually helps the adult to resist children's demands to buy foods with a high sugar content. It is also essential not to tempt children by having sweets and junk foods constantly accessible within the home. Simply refusing to buy the items will ensure that the children will not overindulge in them. Furthermore, most children will not vigorously demand junk food items if given reasonable freedom in choosing from an array of appropriate foods. Although it is advisable to keep unhealthy foods out of the home, children should be allowed to indulge in sweets while participating in certain social events (that is, birthday parties, holiday gatherings, etc.). Denying children specific foods that are an integral part of a social event serves only to dramatically increase their attraction to the foods. Parents who are adamantly opposed to their children's indulgence in junk foods should either keep the children home or take them to the party after such foods have been served. These choices are preferable to establishing an atmosphere of anxiety and tension surrounding the children's eating behavior.

All too often, parents offer food to satisfy children's needs that are not related to hunger or physical nurturance. Food may be used to console a child who is temporarily depressed; to relieve boredom; or as a reward for a job well done. Such misuse of food often results in serious consequences. Children learn to misinterpret various unrelated feelings as hunger, and artificial needs to eat may emerge. Hence the child eats to ward off depression, to relieve boredom, or to achieve a sense of security that is not derived from other sources. Such patterns obviously lead to persistent overeating and eventually result in obesity. Eating problems of that origin are particularly difficult to rectify because the children's overall sense of well-being becomes dependent on the ingestion of food. Such patterns can be avoided by the presentation of food in response to children's signal of hunger, rather than by the application of food as a solution to other problems.

In establishing desirable eating habits, adults should closely examine their roles as models or examples. It is not surprising that children adopt eating behaviors similar to those of significant adults in their environment. Parents should ask themselves the following questions: (1) Do we serve heaping piles of high calorie foods? (2) Do we gulp food down as quickly as possible, while anticipating second helpings? (3) Is food an integral part of most of our enjoyable activities? (4) Do we refuse food when we're not hungry? (5) Do we insist on a "clean plate" before eating dessert or leaving the table? Positive answers to the questions indicate the existence of behaviors and attitudes that are incompatible with teaching desirable eating behaviors to children. A high probability of obesity exists for children whose parents are overeaters.

Exercise and physical activity are critical to any program of weight control. Recent studies show that the amount of exercise is at least as important as eating habits in weight control. Exercise serves the dual function of burning calories and suppressing appetite. Routine exercise is essential to the well-being of all children, particularly those involved in weight control programs.

SUMMARY

I have discussed a number of behaviors that children display and that lie within the behavioral psychologist's area of expertise. The following chapter will focus on answers to common questions presented by parents.

nine

ANSWERS
TO COMMON
QUESTIONS

My thirteen-month-old daughter has begun to play with various items on tables throughout the house. She has broken several decorative items. How should I handle this?

This is a question frequently asked of psychologists by parents of children ranging in age from approximately ten months to two years. Although there are several approaches to the problem of handling and manipulating display pieces, there is certainly a question of personal philosophy. Many parents maintain that children should learn not to handle items on coffee tables in their homes, because such behavior will transfer to other settings—namely, other people's coffee tables.

Many adults attempt to eliminate this type of behavior by

slapping a child's hand. This is an unnecessary and ineffective procedure, with possible adverse side-effects. It would certainly be unfortunate inadvertently to suppress curiosity in a young child. Also, this kind of emotionally laden procedure may serve to reinforce rather than suppress the undesirable behavior.

I prefer a two-pronged approach to the problem: diversion and time-out. A diversion for children may be created by providing a special table that is theirs to use as they please. A miniature table and chairs can be placed in a remote corner. It doesn't have to be an expensive piece of furniture—a cardboard box draped with a tablecloth would adequately serve the purpose. The children would eventually learn to discriminate between appropriate table tops on which to play. I would recommend the time-out procedure to extinguish playing with the wrong items.

Sandy has been bladder-trained for three years. However, she began wetting after her grandfather's death about two months ago. What should I do to retrain her?

The loss of a loved one usually results in an emotional impact that is sometimes characterized by regression. Regression is simply an emotional reaction in which a child falls back on previously dominant emotional responses. Sandy's behavior may be more immature and infantile in a number of ways, other than simply wetting the bed.

Sandy needs support and warmth in her relationships with parents and peers. She needs understandable explanations of death and the ritual that surrounds death in our culture. The bed wetting itself should be de-emphasized unless it persists for several months. It is always helpful to require a child to wash soiled clothes and sheets, and she should be expected to remake the bed. However, she should not be scolded or punished. Consultation with the family physician is recommended if grief is profound and enduring.

John sucks his thumb only while watching television. The habit is annoying to us and we would like it to stop.

I have found that instructing parents simply to walk over and turn off the television is a fairly effective remedy for such behavior. In that way, a time-out procedure is employed that occurs in close temporal proximity to the behavior. A surprisingly large number of parents have reported this problem to me.

I have found our four-year-old playing with a toy that he obviously took from a department store. I am embarrassed and am at a loss about what to do.

The manner in which the situation is managed can be critical to a child's moral development. Most four-year-old children will take items that do not belong to them, although without malicious intent. It is important for a parent to handle the episodes in a calm and straightforward fashion. The child should accompany his parents to the store to return the item. Parents should carefully explain the reasons for not taking items that belong to someone else. Attempts to chastise the child by scolding, moralizing, and so forth, are likely to have adverse effects.

Parents should consult mental health professionals upon suspecting older children of becoming involved in a number of stealing episodes.

Pat throws a temper tantrum whenever she is denied an item at the grocery store. This happens with great frequency and regularity. I usually give in to her tantrum and buy the item that she demands, but I hate to be manipulated this way.

That is a very common example of parents who are losing control of their child. Pat is clearly in control of the parent in the situation and will assuredly continue to throw temper tantrums as long as she is rewarded for them. Children are often very adroit at choosing places and circumstances that will create maximum embarrassment for their parents.

Perhaps the most reliable approach to treating this problem is a preventive approach. The key to preventing temper tantrums is to focus on structuring the situation, such that the child clearly understands what is expected of her. Pat should be told that if she behaves in the prescribed manner she will be rewarded with an inexpensive treat. Once expectations are clearly spelled out, parents have an obligation to enforce them steadfastly. Inconsistencies in the form of failure to follow through on rewards or threats will certainly doom the program to failure.

Temper tantrums may also be avoided by learning to anticipate the situations in which they occur and eliminating the stimuli. For example, many parents find that temper tantrums are more likely to occur before dinner as a partial result of fatigue and hunger. The tantrums may be avoided by providing a light fruit or vegetable snack prior to the time that you anticipate the outburst. On other occasions, you may be able to anticipate the tantrum, but believe that it may not be prevented. That is where coaching and mutual anticipation of the frustrating event can be particularly helpful. Whether or not the outburst can be anticipated, remove the child from the frustrating situation whenever possible.

In summary, good behavior should be spelled out for the child and rewarded frequently and vigorously. Bad behavior in the grocery store should be followed by withdrawal of privileges at home, such as television or dessert. Such behavior could also result in not allowing the child to accompany you on the next outing.

> *Yesterday Steve uttered an obscene word that is unacceptable in our home. I spanked him and he has not uttered the word since.*

The most advisable approach to managing cursing involves simply ignoring the utterances. Scolding and spanking focus too much attention on the undesirable behavior and may supply more fuel to the flame. You state that he has not uttered another obscene word subsequent to the spanking. That may or may not be true as punishment tends to suppress the response only in the presence of the punishing agent. On the other hand, extinguishing the behavior by ignoring it is a more efficient procedure of totally extinguishing the undesirable response.

Jane refuses to play with her cousin, who is the same age. We are a close family and would like the children to have a close relationship. How can we encourage this?

Children, like most adults, can rarely be pushed into congenial relationships. I recommend a relaxed approach in which both children are included in enjoyable activities. It is usually better if the activities require cooperation and interaction, such as putting together an electric train set, making a snowman, and so forth. Such task-oriented activities are excellent for building relationships. Encourage the children to share and to say pleasant things to each other; however, do not get involved in minor squabbles and conflicts. A child may reject the company of another regardless of how the environment is engineered. However, allowing children to develop unique relationships of their own choosing increases the likelihood that they will become friends.

Several older boys have been picking on Walter at school and seriously threatening him. I am afraid for him but don't want to overprotect, because I know that he must fight his own battles.

A young child should not have to fight his own battles against insurmountable odds. A group of boys who are threatening a young child can potentially result in serious emotional and physical wrongdoing to your youngster. Groups of children can sometimes pose a larger threat than individuals because of a number of powerful factors that operate on group behavior. Parents should contact school officials to make certain that their children are closely supervised at all times. Your children should

115

be encouraged to accompany other children whenever moving from one place to another. Parents should encourage the school guidance counselor to investigate the dynamics of the group in order to defuse their malevolent game.

Kim shows no interest whatsoever in school. Although she has the ability to do straight-A work, she is turning in C's and D's.

You are probably aware that academic performance is comprised of ability and motivation to do the work. Even though Kim may be bright and may appear to be intelligent, it is helpful to rule out the possibility that she may possess average to below average ability. Parents are rarely objective evaluators of their children's ability; therefore, it is recommended that objective ability testing be performed. Once you are satisfied that Kim has the ability to make straight A's and your opinion is based at least partially on an objective psychological evaluation, it is wise to develop a specific program that will increase Kim's motivation to do her best work. Most incentive programs involve tokens, contracts, close and frequent monitoring of classroom behavior, praise, encouragement, and material rewards. All these strategies are discussed in this book; however, I recommend professional counseling for the severely apathetic or lethargic student.

You should be constantly aware of the examples that you set for your children. Do you emphasize the intrinsic value of learning? Are trips to museums, art galleries, zoos, and libraries part of your family's recreational activities? Do your children observe you reading frequently? How much of a role do mindless television programs play in your family's leisure time? Your answers to these questions should increase your awareness of the quality of the learning environment that you have created.

Our six-year-old daughter was observed "playing doctor" with a little girl in the neighborhood. We were horrified to discover this and would like to know what it means. Will she be promiscuous? Does she have homosexual tendencies?

116

A vast majority of children from all walks of life engage in exploratory sexual play with peers. Frequently children will choose partners of the same sex, which is considered to be a healthy expression of sexual curiosity. There is absolutely no correlation between childhood play of this nature and adult expressions of sexuality. In other words, there is no basis for the conclusion that your daughter will be either promiscuous or homosexual.

The manner in which parents deal with the situation will largely depend on their personal view of sex and morality. Some parents may choose to ignore innocuous exploratory sexual play, others may gently discourage it, and still others may choose to punish the children. Parents should arrive at individual decisions based on personal feeling and attitudes; however, an overly harsh and punitive approach should be avoided.

> Our son is a poor student and always has been. He is also an excellent athlete and does well in all sports. My husband has threatened to ground him from all participation in sports if his grades don't improve. We need help in settling this issue.

I am opposed to the idea of restricting participation in athletic events based on school performance. Participation in athletics may be the only source of self-esteem for a young person, thus helping that individual to avoid self-destructive delinquent and anti-social behavior. It is my opinion that the best adjusted young people are those who are physically, emotionally, and intellectually fit. Eliminating the opportunity for a young person to participate in athletics would certainly hamper development in those areas.

Perhaps other extracurricular activities, such as television time, overnight guests, movie attendance, allowances, and so forth, should be used as rewards for diligence in school. Taking away the privileges may be very effective punishment for lack of academic diligence.

I would like to qualify my opinion by stating that it may be necessary to restrict the amount of time that is spent in athletics. Many coaches demand virtually all of a young person's free time such that practice may begin to encroach on study time and family time. It may be necessary to reduce the amount of time spent in athletics if that is the case. However, provided that the demands on your child's time are reasonable, he should be allowed to participate fully in the sports of his choice.

I am trying to decide how to administer my child's allowance. Should it be used as a payoff or as an attempt to teach money management? How much should one give children?

I believe that an allowance should be used to teach money management skills, as well as to reward children for fulfilling specific household duties. Such an approach will better prepare your child for effective money management as an adult. Many experts recommend distributing an allowance simply as a tool to teach money management. In my estimation that approach fails to seize the opportunity to teach the child that money must be earned. Therefore, the child will come to expect an allowance regardless of what has been done to earn it. Allow your child some flexibility in determining how the money should be spent so that he/she can learn to make reasoned and thoughtful decisions concerning money use. In that way a child learns that money is a limited resource that should be used wisely.

The amount of money that should be given varies with the age of the child and the financial resources of the family. In considering the sum of the allowance, it is necessary to take into account such factors as cost of necessities and cost of special events. These can be determined by creating a budget for your child on paper that is continuously open for revision. I tend to recommend conservative figures for an allowance, because it is probably more harmful for your child to have too much than too little.

Our son will not eat green vegetables. What should we do?

Perhaps the question can best be answered by recommending what should *not* be done. You should not fight with him over his eating habits. Research has repeatedly determined that children will select nutritious, well-balanced diets over the long run if given a choice. If you think your child is not getting enough of the right kinds of food, it may be wise to consult your pediatrician about the use of supplemental vitamins. Again, it is unnecessary to ruin meals by constantly fighting with your son about his eating habits.

> *Our child is not adjusting well to our recent divorce. I would like to know who would be qualified to help and where I might find such professionals?*

There are several groups of professionals trained to provide effective services for this type of problem. These experts are generally referred to as mental health professionals. Mental health professionals include psychiatrists (physicians with M.D. degrees) and psychologists who hold Ph.D. degrees, in addition to social workers, marriage and family counselors, and pastoral counselors. Most of the professionals in the latter groups have some type of training at the master's degree level.

Usually your safest bet in choosing a competent individual will involve relying on the recommendations of your peers and friends, as well as other professionals. It is necessary to consider expenses involved; services of this nature can be quite expensive. However, most medical insurance policies will cover a substantial portion of the bill that is charged by psychiatrists and psychologists. The services of other mental health professionals are sometimes not included in medical insurance.

You may also find competent mental health professionals in community mental health centers. Such clinics typically prorate their fees based on a client's ability to pay.

EPILOGUE

I have attempted to present a number of useful child-management techniques that have been promulgated by professionals. It would be a glaring error to omit another group of experts—successful parents. The following narrative was printed by the National Institute of Mental Health in its *Plain Talk Series*. I heartily agree with this summary and have found it to be a fitting epilogue for this book.

> *Based upon your personal experiences with your own children, what is the best advice you could give new parents about raising children?*

This question was asked of 50 parents who had "successfully" raised their own children. Their children, all over 21, were considered successful in the sense that they were all productive adults who were apparently adjusting well to our society. Experienced parents are the practitioners who are most likely to know what really works in the home environment.

The results of the survey reveal that there seems to be a common "parent sense" about effective parenting. Although the parents surveyed were mainly from traditional, two-parent families, parents in other circumstances can apply these guidelines to their own situations. For example, single parents or parents in families in which both spouses work may not have a lot of time to spend with their children, but the quality of the time spent—playing and talking with their children and doing things together as a family—is equally important. Similarly, while the parents who were surveyed emphasized the importance of a good marital relationship and the need to spend some time away from their children with their spouses, single parents can foster a healthy personal adjustment by arranging time to be alone or to participate in activities with other adults.

The most frequent responses of the parents are classified under 10 basic principles about which there seems to be general agreement. Although not new, these principles of childrearing can offer a genuinely helpful guide to parents, teachers, day care workers, and others who care for children.

LOVE ABUNDANTLY

The most important task is to love and really care about children. This not only gives children a sense of security, belonging and support, but it also smoothes out the rough edges of childhood. Parental love should be special in two respects. First, it should be constant and unconditional—which means it is *always* present, even when the child is acting in an unlovable manner. Secondly, parents should be open in expressing and showing love so that children are never uncertain about its presence. This means parents should hug and praise their children at every available opportunity.

DISCIPLINE CONSTRUCTIVELY

Discipline means setting and adhering to standards of behavior. After love, the parents stressed the importance of giving clear direction and enforcing limits on a child's behavior. Discipline is an essential preparation for adjusting to the outside world; it makes a child better behaved and happier. It is best to use a positive approach by saying, "*Do* this," more often than "*Don't* do that." Be certain that you punish when you say you will. Be firm by "saying what you mean and meaning what you say." And punish as soon after the misdeed as possible; don't put an extra burden on Dad by saying, "Just wait until your father comes home."

Apart from firmness and immediacy, the parents described the following qualities of constructive discipline:

Be consistent: Don't undermine the rules set by your spouse. Disagreements regarding childrearing must be resolved in privacy—never in front of the children.

Be clear: Establish a few simple rules and spell them out clearly in advance. The child should never be confused about what the rules are.

Administer in private: If possible, never punish a child in front of anyone. This tends to antagonize the child and he or she may continue to misbehave to save face.

Be reasonable and understanding: Explain the reason why a child is being given directions: "The stove is hot, please keep away so you will not be burned." However, don't be afraid to say on occasion, "Do it because I say so." In addition, try to understand a child's point of view and meet him or her halfway. This will give you a closer relationship.

Be flexible: With adolescents, bargaining is an effective tool.

On occasion, it is good for both the parents and the child to be able to bend the rules a little. Also, what works with one child will not necessarily work with another. The child's individual personality enters into it.

Discourage continued dependency: Try to give a child an ever-expanding role in making decisions affecting his or her life. As children reach adolescence, encourage independence, knowing that you have done all you could to form good behavior patterns.

Be authoritative: If you are hesitant or indecisive, or if you feel guilty about disciplining children, you may not do a good job. Remember that you have years of experience, so stick to your decisions. Never let a child talk you out of a punishment you believe necessary. Have the courage to call on and trust your own common sense.

The parents also discussed the type of punishment they found most effective. They said that when a child hurts another person or destroys property, the child should apologize and, when necessary, make restitution from his or her own money. Sending children to their rooms or depriving them of something they enjoy doing was also considered to be a good punishment. Moreover, the parents generally agreed that spanking a young child (i.e., a quick lick on the backside) was OK when necessary. They cautioned that a child should never be beaten, hit on the head, or hit as a means of satisfying parental anger. This finding agrees with most surveys which disclose that most parents (about 85 percent) report that they occasionally spank their children.

SPEND TIME TOGETHER

"Spend lots of time with your children!" was a frequent recommendation. The parents felt that this time should be spent in:

Playing: Spend some time each day playing with the chil-

126

dren. The sole purpose of this play should be enjoyment—not to influence them.

Talking together: Have real conversations with the kids—times when you both listen and sincerely react to one another.

Teaching: Actively teach your children such workaday skills as cooking and car repair.

Encouraging family activities: Family spirit and a sense of belonging are developed by doing things together as a family. Have regular family outings, special family dinners, and spend holidays together. Go to social, sporting, and religious events together. Conduct family council meetings and make decisions together. One parent recommended that families "reduce TV watching by playing family games or by playing musical instruments together." Another said, "You can't fool children by giving them things (toys, TV) rather than your time and attention."

TEND TO PERSONAL AND MARITAL NEEDS

A number of parents specified that personal adjustment was an important first step to effective childrearing. One noted that to relate well to children, adults must be comfortable with themselves. Another parent said that one should not completely sacrifice oneself for the family but rather, "Keep part of yourself for yourself and do something you enjoy." By treating yourself well, this parent felt, you will avoid the feeling of being mistreated, used unfairly, or over-burdened when something goes wrong. A sense of humor about one's faults and the misfortunes of life was also thought to be an important aspect of personal adjustment.

Love, respect, and faithfulness between spouses provide needed security to the family. Two comments by parents seem particularly helpful:

A household in which love is openly expressed is a household in which children flourish. Verbalizing love to one's children is not enough. Parents should make every effort to let their youngsters see warmth and tenderness in their marital relationship. Parents should not underestimate the importance of letting their children know how delighted they are when their spouses enter the house. The morning greeting and the goodnight kiss set an atmosphere which encourages the same kind of affection in the hearts and minds of the children.

A husband and wife are apt to be successful parents when they give their marriage the first priority. It may seem that the children are getting 'second best' from this approach but they rarely are. A happy mother and father are most apt to have happy children when the children's roles are clearly and lovingly defined. Child-centered households produce neither happy marriages nor happy children.

These remarks highlight what many parents are reluctant to admit but what child experts are finding to be true: that children tend to detract from rather than enhance the closeness between husband and wife. Recent studies have shown that a couple's satisfaction with marriage and with each other tends to drop sharply just after their first child is born. With minor variations, it stays at a lower level during the childrearing years and only increases after the youngest child leaves home. Thus, the parents pointed out the need to work at maintaining closeness with a spouse by such means as weekly nights out together, occasional weekends alone together, tender greetings, and thoughtful surprises.

TEACH RIGHT FROM WRONG

A number of the responses highlighted the need for parents to actively teach children basic values and manners in order for them to get along well in society. Parents found the following ways helpful in socializing their children: the assignment of chores and other responsibilities at home; religious affiliation; insistence that the children treat others with kindness, respect, and honesty; emphasis on table manners and other social graces in the home; part-time jobs outside the home when the children were old enough; and the setting of personal examples of moral courage and integrity. The successful parents also stressed that they thought parents should clearly state their own moral values and discuss them with their children.

Specific comments of parents include the following:

> Children should be made aware of proper values—behavioral, financial, and so forth. When they stray, parents should communicate in a manner which encourages the child to listen—do not be permissive or rigid but firm, so the children know exactly where you stand.

> Teach children to respect people, to be honest, and to treat others as they themselves would like to be treated.

> All children have to be taught right from wrong, respect for others and their property, and for older people.

> Teach them the value of *truthfulness.* Time and again I recall telling the children that if they told us the truth about a situation we would do all in our power to help them, for in knowing the real facts we could deal with any misstatements by others. If, however, they lied, we would be unable to be of much help because we couldn't depend on them.

DEVELOP MUTUAL RESPECT

The parents emphasized the need to insist that all family members treat each other with respect. First of all, this means that parents should act in respectful ways to the children. The following behaviors exemplify this respect: politeness to children (saying "Thank you" and "Excuse me"); apologizing to a child when you are wrong; showing an active interest in the children's activities and TV shows; being honest and sincere with children at all times; not favoring one child in the family; following through on promises made; and showing basic trust in a child's character and judgment.

In addition, parents should insist on being treated in a respectful way by the children. If parents treat each other with respect and love, and teach the children to respect their parents, a solid foundation will be laid. Another parent suggested: "Parents should maintain their individuality and cultivate their own interests and talents. The time, feelings, and interests of both parents and children should be respected."

REALLY LISTEN

Parents should really listen to their child, from his or her earliest years—which means giving undivided attention, putting aside one's own thoughts and beliefs, and trying to understand the child's point of view. As one parent stated: "No matter how busy or involved you are, *listen* to your child as a person. Listening means understanding and communicating, not the physical act of hearing." It also means talking your child's language, encouraging the expression of feelings—both good and bad—and allowing the child to show hostility or anger without fear of losing your love.

OFFER GUIDANCE

In offering guidance to children when they have problems, the parents recommended that you be brief—state your thoughts in a few sentences rather than make a speech. They also felt it is helpful to make children understand that, although your door is always open to discuss difficulties, before you will offer solutions you expect them to have thought about the problem and to have tried to come up with possible solutions themselves.

Other thoughts by parents on counseling children were:

Don't force your opinions, likes, dislikes. Offer them strictly as your opinion, not as law.

Forbidden fruit is always so tempting, so play it low-key with undesirable activities, TV shows, etc. Kids will usually respect your opinion if you're honest, and they will tend to follow your guidance unless they just have to find out for themselves.

FOSTER INDEPENDENCE

Recognizing that it is difficult to let children go, the parents advocated gradually allowing them more and more freedom or control over their own lives. By fostering independence you will gain their affection and their respect. Children should be given freedom to make decisions regarding minor matters first; then the areas of decision-making should be expanded gradually.

The parents also observed that children have a continuing need for parental support and encouragement throughout adolescence and young adulthood. As one parent expressed it: "Once your children are old enough, kind of phase yourself out of the picture. But always be near when they need you."

BE REALISTIC

Developing realistic expectations about childrearing was also mentioned. Parents advised that one should expect to make mistakes and to realize that outside influences—such as peer group pressure—will increase as children mature. Parents reaffirmed the saying that childrearing is a series of "tough times and tender moments." One parent remarked: "Don't expect things to go well all the time. Childrearing has never been an easy job; it has its sorrows and heartaches, but it also has its great joys—and this is what makes it all worthwhile."

Parenting indeed is not a simple task, and it is easy to become confused and uncertain at times. The plain old-fashioned "parent sense" expressed here seems sensible and stable compared to the passing fads and theories.

The most important thing that parents in this study learned by experience is that steadfast love must go hand-in-hand with discipline; indeed, one is not truly possible without the other. Moreover, in order to love and discipline most effectively, it is necessary to spend constructive time with the children. It would seem, then, that while adjusting to changing times, it is important for parents to hold fast to these and other basic, unchanging principles of childrearing.

INDEX

progress review, 17-18
promptness of recording, 16-17

Journal of Social Issues, 61, 62

Kagan, J., 51

Labels, problems with, 5-6
and labeler, 6
negative, 6
self-esteem, 5
self-fulfilling prophecy, 6
stigmas, 6
Listening to child, 130
Love, 124-25
Lying. *See* Dishonesty.

Masturbation, 93-94
example, 93
excessive, 93-94
in infants, 93
reactions to, 93
urinary tract, infection of, 94
Money. *See* Allowances.
Motivation
effects, 51
environmental context, 51
goals, setting of, 53
grades, 52
leisure, utility of, 52
nature, 27
rewards for children, 52-53
Mussen, P. H., 51
Mutual respect, 129-30
from adults, 129
from children, 130

National Institute of Mental Health, 123
Negative reinforcements, 32-33
aversive stimuli, 33
avoidance, 33
escape, 33
Newborns. *See* Sibling conflict.
Nightmares, 100-101
example, 100
treatment, 100-101
Noncompliance, 86-87
example, 86
and nagging, 86

strategy for dealing with, 86-87

Obesity, prevention of, 101-104.
See also Food.
breastfeeding, 102-103
commercial milk formulas, 103
and conversion to fat, 102
fat babies, stereotype about, 104
food production, 101
force feeding, avoidance of, 103
modern technology, effects of, 101
prevalence of, 101
stigma of, 102
weight gain, in infants, 103-104

Parenting
general principles about, 123-24
lack of training for, 3-4
Pavlov, Ivan, 94
Personality, early, 27
Plain Talk Series, 123
Playing doctor. *See* Sexual play.
Positive reinforcement
amount, 29
vs. bribery, 32
and children, 28
vs. coaxing, 32
cues, use, 31
delay, 30
diminution of reward, 30, 31
effectiveness of, 29
establishment of behavior, 30-31
immediacy, 30
primary, 28
rewards, anticipation of, 28
secondary, 28
social, 29
timing, 29-30
Privileges, withdrawal of, 65-66
Property, concept of, 113
Proverbs, 61
Punishment, 32, 33, 57-64
aggression, 63
behaviors causing, 59
children, reactions of, to, 63
confusion of with discipline, 57
infants, 61-62
injury, 62
Judaeo-Christian principles, 57
nature, 57